I0033759

ROUTLEDGE LIBRARY EDITIONS:
HISTORY OF EDUCATION

EDUCATION AND THE PROFESSIONS

EDUCATION AND THE PROFESSIONS

EDITED FOR THE
HISTORY OF EDUCATION SOCIETY

BY T. G. COOK

Volume 11

Routledge
Taylor & Francis Group

LONDON AND NEW YORK

First published in 1973

This edition first published in 2007 by
Routledge

2 Park Square, Milton Park, Abingdon, Oxfordshire OX14 4RN

Simultaneously published in the USA and Canada
by Routledge

711 Third Avenue, New York, NY 10017

First issued in paperback 2014

Routledge is an imprint of the Taylor & Francis Group, an informa business

Transferred to Digital Printing 2007

© 1973 History of Education Society

All rights reserved. No part of this book may be reprinted or
reproduced or utilised in any form or by any electronic,
mechanical, or other means, now known or hereafter invented,
including photocopying and recording, or in any information
storage or retrieval system, without permission in writing
from the publishers.

British Library Cataloguing in Publication Data
A catalogue record for this book is available from the British
Library

Library of Congress Cataloging in Publication Data
A catalog record for this book has been requested

ISBN 978-0-415-43239-9 (hbk)
ISBN 978-0-415-76170-3 (pbk)
ISBN 978-0-415-41978-9 (Set)

Publisher's Note
The publisher has gone to great lengths to ensure the quality
of this reprint but points out that some imperfections in the
original copies may be apparent.

HISTORY OF EDUCATION SOCIETY

Education and the Professions

Edited for the Society by
T. G. COOK

METHUEN & CO LTD
11 New Fetter Lane London EC4P 4EE

First published in 1973
by Methuen & Co Ltd
11 New Fetter Lane, London EC4P 4EE
© 1973 by History of Education Society
Typeset by
Preface Limited
Salisbury Wilts
and printed in Great Britain by
Lowe & Brydone (Printers) Ltd
Haverhill Suffolk

SBN 416 78730 4

Distributed in the USA by
HARPER & ROW PUBLISHERS, INC.
BARNES & NOBLE IMPORT DIVISION

Contents

History of Education Society

Chairman	David Bradshaw
	(Principal, Doncaster College)
Vice-Chairman	Professor Brian Simon
	(University of Leicester)
Secretary	E. J. T. Brennan
	(Cambridge Institute of Education)
Conference Secretary	D. Byford
	(Doncaster College)
Treasurer	Trevor Hearl
	(St Paul's College, Cheltenham)
Editor of the Bulletin	T. G. Cook
	(University of Cambridge)
Other Committee Members	Professor W. H. G. Armytage
	(University of Sheffield)
	Professor Kenneth Charlton
	(King's College, University of London)
	Nanette Whitbread
	(City of Leicester College)

The aim of the Society, founded in 1967, is to further the study of the history of education by providing opportunities for discussion among those engaged in its study and teaching.

Conferences and meetings are organized, a bulletin is published twice a year in spring and autumn, a journal, *History of Education*, and other publications pertaining to the history of education are sponsored.

Membership is open to all connected in a professional capacity with education, or engaged in the study or teaching of the history of education. Overseas members are welcomed and are offered a specially reduced subscription rate. Libraries are invited to subscribe to the bulletin only; otherwise Society membership is individual not institutional.

Annual subscriptions	Members	£2
	Overseas members (surface mail)	£1
	Student members	50p
	Libraries	£1
Life membership		£25
Life membership (overseas)		£10

Inquiries about membership of the Society should be addressed to the Secretary, Mr E. J. T. Brennan, Cambridge Institute of Education, Shaftesbury Road, Cambridge, CB2 2BX.

Preface

Educational historians have, as Professor Kenneth Charlton points out in his contribution to this book, been interested in the history of the professions in the past largely through the study of the teaching profession. Recently, however, they have widened their horizons to study how other professions prepared themselves for their work. The professions are closely involved with education. Not only may the process of professional preparation be educative but the professions influence the educational system and in turn are influenced by it. Certainly in England part of the educational system has been based on the preparation of particular professions, while the preparation of some professions has included an element of general education significant in establishing identity and status. 'Education and the Professions' was chosen as the theme of the History of Education Society's annual conference held at the Royal Ford Hall of Didsbury College, Manchester, in December 1972. The papers given by the speakers invited to contribute to the general theme are printed in this book substantially in the form in which they were delivered.

Dr Geoffrey Millerson of the Department of Sociology at the University of Bristol, who has written on the qualifying associations, opened the conference by his paper on 'Education in the professions'. In this he begins by considering how professions separate themselves out from other occupations and goes on to examine the interaction between the needs of professional education and the development of the educational system. On the one hand, the system of education underlies the development and maintenance of a profession. On the other, professional education may be seen as the summit of the educational system. Changes in the educational system may proceed from, and certainly will influence, professional education. This interaction involves a consideration of the structure of education, though, as Dr Millerson also shows, the process of education for the aspiring professional is even more important and interesting as a subject of study and, too, invites further inquiry.

In consequence, in an account of 'The education of the professions in sixteenth-century England', Professor Kenneth Charlton of King's College, London, shows that there was a lack of homogeneity in some sixteenth-century professions and that a relatively common feature of their upper reaches was an insistence that their status derived more from the general education members had received rather than specific professional training. Yet parts of specific training, in the common law, for example, were included as part of the general education of the nobility and gentry in the sixteenth and early seventeenth centuries. The clerical profession, particularly in the seventeenth century, was, paradoxically, faced by those who asserted that formal education was not necessary and could indeed prevent a minister from carrying out his spiritual task.

Of the three papers in the book that deal with the teaching profession, that of Dr Bamford, the Director of the Institute of Education in the University of Hull, considers the nature of the profession of teaching that came into being as the public schools developed in Victorian Britain. Dr Bamford deals with recruitment into the profession and with salary and other signs of professional status. Public school teaching was not homogeneous, so he explores the differences between different schools as well as between head and assistant masters.

It can be argued that the public school master's general education was also his professional training. It was his work for Honours School or Tripos that gave him the knowledge he imparted to his pupils even though he had no training in how to go about this specifically professional part of his task. The training colleges, about whom Dr J. L. Dobson, lately Principal of Padgate College of Education, writes, began by giving specific pedagogical training but developed in addition the general education that can be recognized as contributing to the status of the teacher. The setting-up of day training colleges associated the professional training of teachers with the universities. Dr Dobson draws attention to the growth of this system and its effect on other training colleges up to the point at which the Departmental Committee on the Training of Teachers of 1925 recommended the separation of the training colleges from the universities. The repercussions of this were to last beyond the Second World War to influence recommendations made in the McNair and Robbins Reports.

In the last paper in the book Professor Harold Perkin of the University of Lancaster describes the rise in modern times of the profession of university teachers. In this he shows a fusion between two traditions, the professional, represented first in Britain by the Scottish universities, and the tutorial traditions of Oxford and Cambridge. For Professor Perkin, however, university teaching is not just one new emergent and expanding profession, it is the key profession, that to which all other professions must now look for the supply both of new recruits to their professions and of the new ideas on which the future of our society depends.

The Society is grateful to those who spoke at the conference for agreeing to the inclusion of their papers in this book as well as to Methuen and Co for undertaking its publication and so adding another to the series which now includes *Studies in the Government and Control of Education* (1970), *The Changing Curriculum* (1970), *History, Sociology and Education* (1971) and *Local Studies and the History of Education* (1972). We are again grateful to David Hempsall for preparing the index.

T. G. Cook
University of Cambridge

GEOFFREY MILLERSON

Education in the Professions

In any discussion of the professions it is useful to begin by separating professions from other types of occupations. Such a separation is both important and valuable because professions form a distinctive kind of occupation. Professionals tend to isolate themselves from other types of workers in many ways. Society separates professions from other occupations by according high status, which is demonstrated by prestige and a reward system. In turn, the high status relates to selective recruitment, prolonged training, standards of competence subject to qualification, and some degree of control over members of the occupation. Many of these elements may be found in other occupations, so they do not go far to designate professions.

The essential point in considering professions is that high status is achieved and eventually ascribed. Occupations become professions as a result of deliberate action on the part of occupational members. The notion is dynamic rather than static. The status of a profession is based largely on a claim to specialized knowledge acquired through advanced training and education, although the standing of the profession in the society may, in the end, depend on its assessed value by users and non-users. Occupations undergoing a process of professionalization rely heavily on an ability to raise the level of entry into the occupation and to raise the standard of competence acquired through training and education. There is a very strong link between education and the professions. The educational system affects the professions; in turn, the professions affect the educational system.

Separation of professions from other occupations can be accomplished in a variety of ways: first, by offering a set of characteristics or traits which decide whether or not an occupation can be defined as a profession; secondly by considering whether or not there is evidence of

1

professionalization, i.e. indications that an occupation is making efforts to achieve recognition as a profession; thirdly by developing some model of professionalism which is based on one or more aspects of professional practice or performance.

Analysis of attributes or characteristics of a profession represents a standard, traditional approach to the definition of a profession. Attempts to compare these sets of traits reveal long lists of possible real and ideal categories.[1] Professions are said to possess a widely accepted high status, to involve a prolonged training and education, to be altruistic, to be organized, to be autonomous, to be controlled by ethical codes, and so on. Definition in terms of characteristics has a number of advantages. It provides a simple measuring device to decide whether or not an occupation can be considered a profession, assuming there is some agreement about the characteristics in the first place. It offers some guidance to occupations striving to achieve recognition as professions. It is possible to manipulate the definition to include appropriate elements or exclude inappropriate elements according to the occupation or profession being examined, whether it is one's own profession or that of someone else. On the other hand, this kind of definition suffers many disadvantages.[2] A search for definitions offered by different sources shows a lack of consensus, and lists do not necessarily overlap. The categories in the lists are often not mutually exclusive nor clearly enough defined to distinguish professions from non-professions. Quite frequently, these definitions contain a built-in bias either because they are based on the older professions such as medicine and the law as they were many years ago, or because they are distorted by the selectivity of authors. These definitions do not take into account variations between professions or even within professions. They do not consider the variations between different societies with different social structures and cultures. Perhaps one of the biggest dangers lies in the attempts of occupations to gain the label of profession by means of organizing a qualifying association to satisfy prescribed conditions.[3]

Even attempts to stretch a definition beyond simple categories remain unsatisfactory. W. J. Goode, in a classic paper, tried to identify professions by considering them as a kind of 'community'.[4] He suggested that the professional community was based on a system of shared identity between members, shared values, definitions of professional roles and legitimation by those outside the community. While this idea gets away from the straight designation of characteristics, it still relies heavily upon an old-time professional ideal. It neglects to take into account changes in the professional ideal which result from a variety of social and economic changes. Nevertheless, despite recent continuous criticisms of the trait-set approach to defining professions, it is still used because of convenience, as in the recent investigation by the Monopolies Commission, and it tends to be appreciated by the professions themselves.[5]

A second general method adopted to separate professions is in terms of 'professionalization', the emphasis being placed on the process of an occupation becoming a profession. T. Caplow and H. Wilensky offer two examples of this approach. Wilensky considers that an occupation undergoes professionalization through a series of sequential stages: the creation of a full-time occupation, the establishment of a training school, the formation of a professional association, and lastly the formation of a code of ethics.[6] Caplow presents a slightly different combination and order of events, thus: the formation of a professional organization, the change of the occupational title, the development of an ethical code, the use of political agitation for recognition, and the emergence of training facilities.[7] Wilensky goes further to develop four occupational types based on the degree to which occupations proceed throughout these stages without 'errors or ties'. The classification consists of established professions, marginal professions, new professions and doubtful professions. There is a certain attractiveness in focusing upon the process of professionalization rather than upon a list of ideal characteristics. Occupations do indeed take deliberate action to become professions. They tend to develop a sense of group consciousness resulting from efforts to define their specialism as a basis for full-time work. Often, they will seek a more acceptable and respectable title for the occupation. Organization tends to take place fairly rapidly. The professional association quickly seeks to establish membership as a qualification for demonstrating expertise. They do attempt to gain recognition of the qualification by convincing employers, Government, educational authorities, etc., of the unique value of the qualification.

Does a concentration on the notion of professionalization provide a better solution to the analysis of professions? There are problems. These various stages are not always identifiable or appropriate in considering occupations moving towards professional status for their workers. The different stages and the resultant typology tend to be biased against occupations seeking to achieve professional status. They tend to ignore the relationship between occupations and the wider society. More sophisticated efforts to develop a separation of professions by constructing an index of professionalization also seem to prove unsatisfactory. D. J. Hickson and M. W. Thomas have demonstrated this, using data derived from forty-three qualifying associations to calculate scores of professionalization.[8] They were able to show that older organizations have larger scale-scores than newer associations, demonstrating a more advanced stage of professionalization. Using the process of professionalization as an indicator of eventual professional status is not yet a certain approach to the separation of professions from other occupations. It tends to fall back on to some definition of goals. If an occupation aims to become a profession, what does it aim for? Is there only one way of becoming a profession? How do members of an occupation know when they have reached the required level to be accepted as professionals?

A third way of analysing professions is to compare them with some model of professionalism. These models do not define professions, in fact, they tend to assume separation and to concentrate on the value of the professions in providing a service to the community. More often than not, they stress the altruistic nature of the service, the selfless dedication of the professional to the needs of others. R. H. Tawney and T. H. Marshall both offer examples of this view, which can be traced back to the work of Durkheim writing in the late nineteenth century. In a general critique of modern society, Tawney attacked the notion of functionless property in the capitalist system.[9] His idea for reorganization was the subordination of industry to the needs of the community based on a comparison of industry and the professions. He presents an idealistic model of professionalism. Professions serve others unselfishly, industry should do the same. Marshall in his evaluation of changes in professions stresses that the essence of professionalism is the welfare of the client rather than professional self-interest.[10] In the United States, numerous attempts have been made to compare business standards and professional standards.[11] These comparisons between professional ethics and business practice rely on the model of the selfless service of the professional contrasted with the profit-making, competitive, self-interested ideals of business. This kind of comparison makes it difficult for managers to lay claim to professional status. More recently, professions have been accused of blatant self-interest, while the Monopolies Commission revealed a number of restrictive practices which tarnish the professional image.[12] However, P. Halmos has returned to the noble ideal of the professions, stressing the moral value.[13] Like Durkheim, he sees professions as exerting a moral influence in society through their altruism.

To some extent, the model of the professional ideal can be tested by an examination of actual professional practice, or even the tenets which professional organizations offer to guide the professional.[14] Analysis of professional ethics suggests that ethical codes, if they do exist, are concerned more with the protection of the professional than with the client. Codes tend to protect the professional from the client. They are often more concerned with preserving the professional image than with exposing incompetence or professional failure. Altruism in the professional ideal has always been tempered with a desire to extract the maximum reward for services which a client may, or may not, be able to provide for himself. Professional status in the community depends on ability to earn high rewards rather than on the simple provision of service.

Another recent interesting model of professionalism has been put forward by T. J. Johnson.[15] He develops a model based on a producer–consumer relationship arising from the supply of any kind of service. In this producer–consumer relationship, Johnson considers there are three broad areas of conflict. First, where the producer defines the needs of the consumer and the means by which the needs are to be catered for. This is called collegiate control, and it is usually accompanied by the emergence of autonomous occupational associations (professions come under this category). Secondly, where the consumer defines his own needs and the means by which the needs are met. (This type is called patronage.) Finally, where a third party mediates in the relationship between the producer and the consumer, defining the needs and the manner in which these needs are met. (This is called mediative.)

This typology, and the base on which it rests, focuses directly on the supply of and the demand for service. It goes further to relate professions to the power structure in society. It provides a useful compromise which allows for variations within and between professions, by considering the nature of the service provided and control over provision. However, the model does not take into account the career development of the professional and the more interesting problem of differentiation within professions through training and control. It tends to be a disguised return to an analysis based on professional service. Perhaps this does not advance much further than Parson's analysis of the professional–client relationship.[16]

Summarizing these various methods of separating professions from other occupations, several essentials seem to emerge. In the first place, any attempt to separate professions must consider professions which are established and recognized, taking into account both their structure and their operation. The analysis must also include an examination of the process by which occupations become professions. It must, moreover, involve a discussion of the professional in the work situation. Lastly, it should consider the determinants or bases for the subjective and objective recognition of the profession. In the end, it is possible to isolate factors which contribute to successful professionalization: ability to achieve a definable basis of background knowledge and practice, plus a crystallization of the activities composing the occupational task; opportunity to acquire knowledge and practice; the development of self-consciousness by emerging professionals; realization and recognition of the occupation as a profession by those outside the occupation.

Underlying the development and maintenance of the profession is the system of education. But any account of education in the professions must allow for two important aspects of the provision: the interaction between professions and the educational system and the pattern of education within individual professions seen as a continuous process. The analysis must relate individual professions to the general structure of the wider educational system. It must look at the total ongoing process within the individual professions. It must take note of the relation between the educational processes in different professions. The educational system in Britain has always, to some extent, been dependent upon the demands or needs of professional education. Equally, professions have been subject to the development and inbuilt limitations of the wider educational system.

Investigation of the system of professional education leads to the distinction between structure and process. The structure of education is concerned with the position of professional education and training relative to the total educational system — the institutions, the teaching methods, curricula, and so on. The process of education is more properly associated with the continuous development of the professional and is more accurately described as professional socialization. Looking at the structure of professional education and the interaction between professional training and the total educational system, two broad patterns seem apparent: professions developing within the educational system; and, as a result of changes in the educational system, professions almost independently developing methods outside the established educational system.

Looking at the British educational system as a whole, several important changes have taken place since the beginning of the nineteenth century. There has been, first of all, a gradual and definite interlocking of the systems of primary, secondary and tertiary or higher education which has affected patterns of entry, curricula, teaching methods, etc. Education has largely come to mean some form of institutional training. There has also been a move to almost complete dependence upon written examinations as the main criteria of success at each stage in the system. An academic education leading to a university degree has become the true goal, the ultimate culmination of educational experience. These broad changes have had a number of effects on occupations in general and upon professions in particular.

In the first place, opportunity has increased for specialization in education leading to specific expertise and greater occupational differentiation. Next, there has been a move from a reliance on practical training and experience as a means of acquiring expertise towards a strongly academic, theoretical base. Thirdly, there has been a reduction in occupational self-recruitment and an increasing openness or freedom of entry into skilled occupations and professions for a wider section of society. Fourthly, a succession of barriers or hurdles have been built at different stages in the educational process which must be overcome if one is to qualify for admission to subsequent stages and eventual recognition of competence. Success at different barriers gives differential access to occupations. Fifthly, progress through the educational system gradually restricts the choice of occupational careers, because alternatives open or close at different stages or levels in the educational system. Lastly, the educational system has become the main means of access to high-status occupations and to social mobility in society, providing a safer, more certain method of achievement.

As an example of these effects, it is possible to cite the medical profession.[17] At the beginning of the nineteenth century, there were a few unimportant qualifications available; education was mainly in the form of practical training through apprenticeship, practice was largely undifferentiated, and there was limited contact or overlap with other professions or specialisms. Today, there is increasing sub-specialization and intensive expertise and a move away from an emphasis on general practice; there is greater interaction with other kinds of specialists (academics, administrative personnel, technologists and technicians, researchers); there are more clearly defined career patterns which restrict transfer; and there is an emphasis on a strong academic and theoretical base which is acquired only at university medical schools. These changes in the medical profession do, in part, represent a response to increased medical knowledge, redefinitions of work and attempts to consolidate status, but they have also been affected by the above-mentioned changes in the educational system.

Taking the development of professions as a whole, some were able to fit into the existing structure of the educational system as the system developed; other professions were able to adapt the educational system to fit their needs; yet other professions were forced to develop their educational structures outside the system.[18] In the early nineteenth century, the accepted professions of law, medicine and the Church did not rely on certification following elaborate theoretical instruction, although aspirant professionals were dependent on recognition by controlling authorities. But these authorities required only limited evidence of competence, only attachment to traditional forms of training. Barristers were expected to become students of an Inn of Court, eat dinners and to attend the ritual practice of moots or mock trials, possibly visiting courts to see the law in action. Clergy of the Church of England were not required to undertake courses in theology or show successful completion of any courses taken. Doctors could attend some form of training in hospitals and in private medical schools, but qualifications were not insisted upon before practice. While the universities of Oxford and Cambridge provided degrees in medicine and the Royal Colleges of Physicians and Surgeons offered membership as qualifications, these measures of tested competence, such as they were, did not seem to be readily sought or expected. Only in the central area of London was there some restriction over practice exercised by the Royal College of Physicians.

Professions attempting to establish themselves in the first half of the nineteenth century were faced with a limited, uneven system of primary education, a rudimentary form of secondary education mainly catering for the middle-class functionless gentlemen of the future and an archaic underdeveloped structure of higher education. Unable to rely or build upon State provision of basic education, three solutions were adopted by newly formed associations of practitioners. Some, like the doctors and veterinary surgeons, strengthened existing training facilities and organized examinations. A second group, including pharmacists and actuaries, provided examinations and specially organized tuition.

Others, such as the solicitors, architects and engineers, relied on a traditional system of apprenticeship or pupilage with or without examinations.

Developments since the mid-nineteenth century have proved crucial for the emergence of professions and the expansion of further and higher education in Britain. For emerging professions, a means appeared by which occupations could transform themselves and lay claim to recognition as professions. They could form a qualifying organization. These organizations of practitioners adopted a structural framework and methods of operation similar to those pioneered by earlier associations of engineers, architects, pharmacists and actuaries. To create confidence among users of their services in the competence of their members, they set examinations. The idea of tested competence and an acceptable level of experience in the work generated real educational problems. First, setting professional examinations depended upon the provision of a basic standard of preliminary general education at a lower level, but the national system of elementary and secondary education was initially unreliable and only slowly transformed. Secondly, the numbers of students and candidates for examinations were small and indeterminate. Thirdly, curricula could not be devised because the nature and content of applicable courses was uncertain. Fourthly, there was a need to reconcile a demand for practical experience with the requirements of theoretical knowledge. Lastly, suitable teachers and teaching materials had to be found for instructing students and methods devised for preparing them for specialized examinations.

Demands made for the provision of professional training and education over the last hundred years have tended to create problems of provision in further and higher education. The growth of institutionalized training and education in the national system of education did not fully take into account the needs of professions. University expansion and development tended to follow a traditional pattern of higher education built up from the Middle Ages, offering inappropriate courses which were almost entirely non-vocational. Except for medicine, science, engineering and to some extent law, most universities developing from the late nineteenth century showed a reluctance to introduce subject-areas related to newer professions. Universities hesitated to provide facilities for teaching accountancy, elements of commercial practice, librarianship and various technological subjects. The failure of universities to show interest in courses required by newer

B

professions forced many professions to turn to institutions outside universities and particularly towards technical colleges and colleges of commerce. Occasionally, they were forced to set up their own teaching institutions.[19] Where institutional provision could not be made, professions became more or less completely dependent on correspondence tuition.[20] The general effects on the educational system have been widespread. One important result has been the failure over the years to develop an integrated system of further and higher education, offering an adequate supply of places to cater for demand. A further consequence has been the introduction of a status hierarchy in institutions, classifying, segregating and evaluating different kinds of provision. It has also led to the growth of a dependence in professional education on part-time evening or correspondence tuition. Finally, it has increased the difficulty of assessing the value of different qualifications.

Professions seeking a system of training and education have had to promote their own standards and to depend largely on their ability to adapt to existing arrangements. This dilemma has produced real difficulties for many professions. Qualifying associations have been forced to use limited resources to produce their own teaching materials, to set examinations and to supervise teaching arrangements. Separate provision by different organizations has often resulted in over-specialization and unnecessary proliferation of qualifications. Inadequate and insufficient provision has tended to foster high wastage and failure rates among students and possibly to cast doubts on the value of the eventual qualification.

Professions today can be divided roughly into three groups: registered professions controlled by statute; professions in which certain kinds of work are controlled by statute; professions in which practice is not controlled in any way by law.[21] Going further into professional education, training and qualification may be grouped into approximately four types: (1) the requirement of a university training including practical work spread over a prolonged period of time (doctors, veterinary surgeons, dentists); (2) a university degree or equivalent, with full-time or part-time education and training over an extended period (engineers, architects); (3) no full-time means of qualification, but a period of full-time sandwich courses (accountants, solicitors); (4) no full-time means of qualification, with education provided by evening classes, day release or correspondence tuition without the requirement of formal training.

So, at one end of the spectrum, there are registered professions with education and training based on an institution and qualification mainly in terms of university degrees. At the other end, there are professions uncontrolled by law in any way, relying on non-institutional education and training with qualifications probably not equivalent to degree level. Investigation by the Robbins Committee considered the full range of education and training in higher education.[22] Subsequent action and policy changes have not contributed to any real rationalization of training and education for the professions. The only sign of modification appears to be the recent White Paper which mainly affects teacher training and the general provision of higher education.[23] Much greater attention should be paid to the integration of systems of training, education and examinations. Standards need to be made more uniform. Too much reliance is placed on the ability of professions to regulate themselves and to find some means of co-operation for themselves. Notable exceptions, such as the Council of Engineering Institutions and the Four Societies of the Land, demonstrate the ability of some professional organizations to co-operate and to rationalize their own procedures. On the other hand, there have been many examples of organizations failing to join together in common interest or to go beyond partial co-operation.[24] This leads to inefficiency, uneven standards and unreliable measures of professional competence.

So far, emphasis has been placed on some of the issues arising from the interaction between professional education and the general educational system. However, the structure of education is only part of any discussion of professional education; even more important and interesting is the process of education for the professional.

In the study of professional education, most attention has been paid to the problems of the professional passing through a period of training to reach a recognized, acceptable level of competence. Four phases can be identified in the total pattern of training and education: recruitment; induction; initiation; maintenance.

Recruitment to the professions is on the whole an unexplored area. A few studies have attempted to examine the extent to which professions are self-recruiting (i.e. children following their parents' professions).[25] Others have investigated changes in the social-class origins of recruits to professions.[26] The limited amount of research on the latter subject tends to show that the general increase in educational opportunity has also increased the chances of working-class children entering the professions. Middle-class children, however, still retain an advantage through their greater likelihood of continuing in secondary education and gaining access to higher education. Some professions may be more difficult for the working-class child to enter because of cost of training and difficulty of becoming established once qualified (e.g. law and stockbroking). Professions connected with commerce, science, engineering, surveying and certain forms of administration may be easier to enter because of the option to qualify while working.

Some professions show relatively high levels of self-recruitment, namely law, medicine, the Church and teaching. This may be related partly to special access through parental connections with educational institutions, as may happen in the case of medicine. Self-recruitment may also occur simply because the children of particular professionals may possess a greater knowledge of the work-situation and greater identification with the work-role. Being the child of a doctor provides a greater insight into the role of doctor through constant contact with professional practice. Knowledge or lack of knowledge of the range of possible professions helps or hinders the ability to choose between them. Knowledge is acquired through subjects taught in schools, direct contact with established professionals, and publicity about requirements for entry, conditions of training, method of qualification and rewards. In addition, admission to training depends increasingly on the ability to gain access to and to perform successfully within the general educational system.

Induction into the profession refers to the process of training and education. As already indicated, this may take place in a number of different ways. It may be full-time or part-time or a mixture of both. It may last a short or long time, spread over three years or more. It may require instruction within the institution or not; in addition, there may be a limited number of available institutions. It may include practical training or not. It may or may not allow for possible modifications in future career patterns. These are all structural limitations or constraints built into the formal system.

Undergoing training and education involves something more for the aspirant professional. The student-professional goes through a period of professional socialization. During training and education, the aspirant professional learns the necessary skills, knowledge and interests required for professional practice. The student acquires the values, the beliefs, the attitudes and assumptions associated with the right and wrong ways of behaving as a professional. This may require unlearning previous patterns of behaviour and extending existing ones. The teaching may intentionally or unintentionally transmit definitions of ways of behaving. The student learns to identify with the professional task. The object of professional socialization is to create a conformity to the norms or rules, the values and expectations about role behaviour as a doctor, lawyer, accountant, teacher, and so on. The student learns through contact with teachers, with peers, with established professionals. The instruction is both formal and informal. It is both verbal and non-verbal. It involves interaction and feedback between students and teachers, students and students, teachers and teachers. In learning to become a particular kind of professional, the student not only acquires skills and an ability to apply skills to solve problems of practice but also learns professional identification and internalizes sets of expectations. The doctor develops a sense of the expectations that a patient may have in seeking advice; at the same time the doctor has a notion of the ways the patient should behave in seeking advice.

A thorough analysis of the process of professional socialization is both complex and in some ways controversial. The number of studies of particular professions is limited. The range of research is restricted. Some of the best studies relate to medicine, nursing, law and teaching.[27] These are not always directly applicable to other professions on account of special circumstances such as length of training, institutional setting, particular professional–client problems and extent of control over the actual work situation. Often contradictions or differences in interpretation make it difficult to give firm statements on agreed mechanisms.

The third stage in professional education and training is the *point of qualification*. As a result of examination, the aspirant professional is adjudged to be competent to practice. The student is initiated into the profession. In most cases, a final examination after a period of training leads to certification. This status passage, theoretically, occurs instantly. A few professions require evidence of practice after final examinations before giving approval of competence as in the case of doctors and barristers. Some professions require practical training as part of the education leading to a final examination, as with solicitors, nurses, architects and chartered accountants. Many professions leave the professional to seek practical training after qualification.

Another problem occurs in relating education, training and qualification to actual practice. It may be that education and qualification are unsuitable for eventual practice, or only partly suitable in terms of the subject-matter of the course. Even worse, there may be little or no instruction in the problems of professional practice and professional ethics. Examples of incomplete or inappropriate training and qualification can be found in a number of professions. Until comparatively recently, medical schools paid very little attention to the problems of environmental and social conditions related to preventive medicine. Equally, training tended to be geared to the career pattern of those seeking to practise physical medicine and surgery in hospitals, despite the fact that most students qualifying end up in general practice.

The last and continuing phase in professional education concerns the *maintenance* of professional competence and integrity. Qualification is not the end. Professional practitioners need to refresh knowledge, to acquire new knowledge, to become aware of changing problems, to develop an awareness of ethical problems. Professionals may also encounter new problems in relation to different aspects of their own work, in relation to their working with others, in relation to working within organizations. Some aspects of their work may overlap with the work of other professionals – which produces problems of encroachment and temptations to give or receive 'kickbacks'. Some professionals may carry several professional roles; for example, a doctor may be a university teacher, a hospital consultant, a researcher and an administrator. Help to overcome problems of adaptation to new knowledge, the difficulties of inter- and intra-professional relationships and professional–client relations could be provided through organizations, suitable literature and specialized courses. The little available evidence suggests that professionals do not always find suitable opportunities for discussion and satisfactory sources of information. Unwillingness to organize activities is often due to over-work, but more often due to apathy of members of the profession. Participation in discussion and a desire to keep up with the subject dissipates with age and experience, together with a feeling of inapplicability to a personal work-situation.

Any discussion of professional education must demonstrate an awareness of the fact that it forms part of the general structure of education. Indeed, in many ways, professional education is the summit of the educational system. The strengths and weaknesses of professional education depend on the past, present and future nature and development of the educational system at the secondary and tertiary levels. Such a discussion has to recognize several essential features of professions. First, the concept of profession is dynamic rather than static – occupations become professions. Secondly, the structure and work of professions change over time in response to the wider changes in society and the changing needs of those within the profession. Thirdly, different professions may well be very different in their recruitment, their types of training and education, their level of qualification, their control over practice.

In the future, although there is a need to recognize the basic autonomy of individual professions, greater efforts must be made to encourage co-operation among them. Furthermore, it is necessary to rationalize and co-ordinate educational facilities, both to improve the standards of competence of professionals and to guarantee a satisfactory level of service to users.

Notes

1   See, for example: G. Millerson, *The Qualifying Associations* (London, Routledge and Kegan Paul, 1964), pp.3–5; E. Greenwood, 'Attributes of a profession', *Social Work*, 2 (1957), pp.45–55; M. L. Cogan, 'The problem of defining a profession', *The Annals* (*Annals of the American Academy of Political and Social Science*), 290 (1955), pp.105–11.
    Definitions of 'profession' based on characteristics can be found in Millerson, op. cit. pp.9–10; A. M. Carr-Saunders and P. A. Wilson, *The Professions* (Oxford, Clarendon Press, 1933); R. Lewis and A. Maude, *Professional People* (London, Phoenix House, 1952).
2   Examples of definitions through occupational interests: H. S. Drinker, *Legal Ethics* (New York, Columbia University Press, 1953); J. L. Carey, *Professional Ethics of Certified Public Accountants* (New York, American Institute of Accountants, 1956); Sir Harold Howitt, 'The profession of accountancy', *The Accountant*, 122 (1950), pp.537–40.
3   The 'qualifying association' is a type of organization which aims to qualify individuals for practice in a particular occupation. There are approximately 180 of these bodies in England and Wales today (see Millerson, op. cit.). Also, Monopolies Commission, *Professional Services*, Part II (London, H.M.S.O., 1970), Cmnd. 4463.
4   W. J. Goode, 'Community within a community: the professions', *American Sociological Review*, 22 (1957), pp.194–200. Further developments of Goode's ideas appear in: W. J. Goode, 'Encroachment, charlatanism and the emerging profession: psychology, sociology and medicine', *American Sociological Review*, 25 (1960), pp.902–14; chapter in A. Etzioni (ed.), *The Semi-Professions and their Organization* (New York, Free Press, 1960). See also a critique in R. Bucher and A. Strauss, 'Professions in process', *American Journal of Sociology*, 66 (1961), pp.325–34.
5   Examples of criticisms of the 'trait approach' to defining professions: R. W. Habenstein, 'A critique of "profession" as a

sociological category', *Sociological Quarterly*, 4 (1963), pp.291–300; W. E. Moore, *The Professions: Roles and Rules* (New York, Russell Sage Foundation, 1970), Ch. 1; T. J. Johnson, *Professions and Power* (London, Macmillan, 1972), pp. 23–32.

6   H. Wilensky, 'The professionalization of everyone', *American Journal of Sociology* (1964), pp.137–58. See also H. W. Vollmer and D. Mills, 'Some comments on "The professionalization of everyone" ', *American Journal of Sociology*, 70 (1965), p.481.

7   T. Caplow, *The Sociology of Work* (Minneapolis, University of Minnesota Press, 1954), pp.139–40.

8   D. J. Hickson and M. W. Thomas, 'Professionalization in Britain: a preliminary measure', *Sociology*, 3 (1969), pp.37–54. Richard Hall developed scales of professionalism by administering attitude scales to different professional groups: R. M. Hall, *Occupations and the Social Structure* (Englewood Cliffs, N.J., Prentice-Hall, 1969), pp.82–91. G. Harries-Jenkins offers a list of 'elements of professionalization', Ch.3 ('Professionals in Organizations'), in: J. A. Jackson (ed.) *Professions and Professionalization* (Cambridge, University Press, 1970), Sociological Studies 3. Ronald Pavalko presents an occupation–profession model which shows professions lying on a continuum built around eight characteristics of work: R. M. Pavalko, *Sociology of Occupations and Professions* (Itasca, Ill., Peacock, 1971), Ch.2.

9   R. H. Tawney, *The Acquisitive Society* (London, Allen and Unwin, 1972), pp.106–11.

10   T. H. Marshall, *Sociology at the Crossroads* (London, Heinemann, 1963), Ch.6 (originally a paper published in 1939).

11   See *The Annals* (*Annals of the American Academy of Political and Social Science*) (May 1922; January 1955; January 1966). Two early examples are: E. L. Heermance, *The Ethics of Business* (New York, Harper and Row, 1926); C. F. Taeusch, *Professional and Business Ethics* (New York, Holt, 1926).

12   For example: D. S. Lees, *The Economic Consequences of the Professions* (London, Institute of Economic Affairs, 1966); Monopolies Commission, *Professional Services* (London, H.M.S.O., 1970), 2 parts, Cmnd. 4462–3.

13   P. Halmos, *The Personal Service Society* (Cardiff, Welsh University Press, 1966). Gross also stresses the importance of attitudinal components in determining the nature of professions: E. Gross, *Work and Society* (New York, Crowell, 1958).

14   See, for example: Millerson, op. cit. pp.165–70, 175–8; Monopolies Commission, op. cit. Part II, Appendices 15, 16; D. S. Lees, *Economic Consequences of the Professions* (London, Institute of Economic Affairs, 1966); R. Klein and A. Shinebourne, 'Doctors' discipline', *New Society*, 22 (528) (1972), pp. 390–401.

15   T. J. Johnson, *Professions and Power* (London, Macmillan, 1972).

16   T. Parsons, 'The professions and social structure', in *Essays in Sociological Theory*, 2nd ed. (New York, Free Press, 1954). Also: *The Social System* (New York, Free Press, 1951).

17   Two useful accounts of changes in medical education are: C. Newman, *The Evolution of Medical Education in the Nine-*

teenth Century (London, Oxford University Press, 1952); F. N. L. Poynter (ed.), *The Evolution of Medical Education in Britain* (London, Pitman, 1966).

18 Millerson, op. cit. pp.120–9.

19 The Pharmaceutical Society set up a School of Pharmacy which eventually became part of London University in 1948. The 'College of Estate Management' was developed by the Chartered Auctioneers and Estate Agents Institute just after the First World War. Other examples can be found. See Millerson, op. cit. pp.133–4.

20 See Millerson, op. cit. pp.140–1; Committee on Higher Education, *Higher Education* (Robbins Report), Appendix Two (B), Part V, Section 1, pp.377–85; also Annex BB (London, H.M.S.O., 1963), Cmnd. 2154 II-I.

21 Millerson, op. cit. pp.88–94; Monopolies Commission, *Professional Services* (1970), Part II.

22 Committee on Higher Education, *Higher Education* pp.166–7, Appendix Two (B).

23 *Education: A Framework for Expansion* (London, H.M.S.O., 1972), Cmnd. 5174.

24 The 'Council of Engineering Institutions' is a body set up in 1962 to co-ordinate examinations and educational policy for over a dozen engineering institutions. The six qualifying associations connected with the 'land' profession (i.e. estate agents, valuers, auctioneers and surveyors) have always worked closely together. An attempt to form an organization like the 'Council of Engineering Institutions' failed after a short experiment. The main accountancy associations have tried several times to amalgamate without success. The last occasion was in 1972. See Millerson, op. cit. pp.202–4.

25 Examples of some studies showing self-recruitment among professions are: R. K. Kelsall, 'Self-recruitment in four professions', Ch.11 in D. V. Glass (ed.), *Social Mobility in Britain* (London, Routledge and Kegan Paul, 1954); Royal Commission on Medical Education, *Report* (Todd Report), Appendix 19 (London H.M.S.O., 1968), Cmnd. 3569; A. P. M. Coxon, *A Sociological Study of the Social Recruitment and Selection of Anglican Ordinands*, Unpublished Ph.D. (Leeds, 1965); R. K. Merton *et. al.*, *The Student Physician* (Cambridge, Mass., Harvard University Press, 1957).

26 Some examples are: R. R. Kelsall, *Higher Civil Servants in Britain* (London, Routledge and Kegan Paul, 1955); W. L. Guttsman, *The British Political Elite* (London, MacGibbon and Kee, 1963); J. Floud and W. Scott, 'Recruitment to teaching in England and Wales', Ch.37 in A. H. Halsey *et al.*, *Education, Economy and Society* (Glencoe, New York, Free Press, 1961); D. H. J. Morgan, 'The social and educational background of Anglican bishops – continuities and changes', *British Journal of Sociology*, XX (3) (1969), pp.295–310; C. B. Otley, 'The social origins of British Army officers', *Sociological Review*, 18 (2) (1970); A. P. M. Coxon, 'Patterns of occupational recruitment: the Anglican ministry', *Sociology*, 1 (1) (1967), pp.73–9.

27   Examples: R. K. Merton, *The Student Physician* (Cambridge, Mass., Harvard University Press, 1957); H. S. Becker, *Boys in White* (Chicago, University of Chicago Press, 1961); M. Janowitz, *The Professional Soldier* (New York, Free Press, 1960); U. Olesen and E. W. Whittaker, *The Silent Dialogue* (San Francisco, Jossey-Bass, 1968); S. Warkov, *Lawyers in the Making* (Chicago, Aldine, 1965).

KENNETH CHARLTON

The Education of the Professions in the Sixteenth Century

In every university there are to be found members of staff who are addressed as Dr Smith, Dr Williams, and so on. These are not medical practitioners but Doctors of Philosophy who work, however, not in a department of philosophy but in, say, a department of chemistry, calling themselves 'chemists'. If, however, they are presented with a National Health Service prescription they would not only be unable to dispense it but they would send the bearer packing to an inferior being, called a pharmacist, who far from holding a higher degree of a university called a doctorate may not even hold a university degree at all – and yet pharmacy is, rightly, regarded as one of the professions. Similarly, in a hospital, the person in charge of the operating theatre would be referred to by his assistants as Mr Johnson, because he is a surgeon, and it would not be until drugs of some kind were needed that the patient would find himself being treated by Dr Wilkinson – a physician, who like Dr Smith the chemist is neither philosopher nor pharmacist.

The explanation of this curious usage is of course to be found in the history of the professions. The historian of education has been interested in the matter in the past, largely through the study of the history of the teaching profession. In recent years, however, he has widened his horizons to make a study of the ways in which other professions, the doctors, the lawyers, the clerics, and so on, have prepared themselves for their work. I want to take a look here at some sixteenth-century professions and their professional preparation. But before I do so I should like to report that when I mentioned the title of this paper to a colleague recently his immediate reaction was to ask '*Were* there professions in the sixteenth century?' – a good historical question which cannot be answered, however, without first clearing up

19

a prior point, which is that it depends what you mean by 'profession', or rather to put it more precisely, it depends what you *count* as a profession, which is not a historical question but a philosophical question, or at least a semantic question. So there is a semantic problem to consider as well as a historical question to answer. But whilst it is useful – indeed essential – to ponder this semantic problem, this problem of definition, the procedure is not without its dangers for the historian, who might fall into the error of considering the problem in twentieth-century terms and then imposing these on his sixteenth-century context. It is important, therefore, to make sure that the semantic clarification remains but a means to an end, the end of seeking historical answers to such questions as: did sixteenth-century practitioners consider themselves members of a profession? did they discuss their work in professional terms? did they use the term 'profession' at all? But we have also to remember that our inquiry is not complete if we inquire simply whether the practitioners used the term and claimed professional status for themselves. We need also to inquire whether such status was accorded to a particular group, either by other professional groups or by society at large. I can only hope in the space allowed to raise some issues and offer some limited exemplification. And I shall limit my examples to the professions of doctor, lawyer, cleric and teacher. There still remains a good deal of work to be done on each of these, but the field is almost virgin when it comes to the emergent professions such as architect, land surveyor, navigator, mapmaker, engineer, and so on.[1]

Originally the term 'profession' simply meant or was used simply to mean a public declaration or vow. But during the medieval period the usage was extended to include any business or occupation which was publicly offered. By the sixteenth century, however, there was a tendency to give the term a narrower and more specialized meaning to apply to a group which though offering a public service did so through a relationship between a principal and a client. This service required a particularized form of knowledge and skill with some theoretical basis, which had been obtained through a fairly lengthy period of study in an institution of higher learning, which institution sometimes, though not always, acted as a qualifying association. In addition this narrower and more specialized meaning of the term 'profession' was reserved for those who by virtue of their membership, knowledge and skill achieved a relatively high social status, sometimes, but not always, measured in terms of monetary reward.

It is remarkable that this sixteenth-century usage has over the centuries acquired its own mystique, so that in 1839 no less a person than Frederic Denison Maurice could claim that 'profession in our country is expressly that kind of business which deals primarily with men as men and is thus distinguished from a trade, which provides for the external wants or occasions of men.'[2] And the ultimate accolade was accorded by the Commissioners of Inquiry into the University of Oxford in 1852, when having made certain recommendations about the reform of teaching in the university they concluded 'a professorship would then . . . become a recognized profession'.[3] If, however, we use such general terms as 'the medical profession', 'the clerical profession', 'the legal profession', 'the teaching profession', an excursion into their sixteenth-century manifestations very quickly draws attention to the heterogeneity of these groups, to the hierarchies into which these groups fell, to the differential status accorded to their membership, and this heterogeneity is to be found as much within the professions as between them.

In the medical profession, for example, a very sharp distinction was drawn by the members of the profession themselves between the physician on the one hand, and the barber surgeons, the apothecaries and the herbalists on the other. Similarly in the legal profession one has to distinguish between on the one hand the civil and canon lawyers (a dying race in this country, though not on the Continent) and the common lawyers, and within those dealing in the common law a very sharp distinction between the barristers and the solicitors, attorneys, notaries, and those stewards of manorial courts who kept the manorial records. Again in the teaching profession at the top of the tree one would find the university teacher, whose function changed quite remarkably in the sixteenth century. Most of the boys who found their way to university would have been taught by the masters and ushers of the endowed grammar schools. But the admissions registers of the colleges also reveal others who had been taught their Latin grammar and literature by private schoolmasters, a group hitherto neglected by historians, largely because so few records of their 'schools' (indeed of their existence) have survived. This latter group of teachers must, however, be distinguished from two other kinds of private school-teacher. On the one hand were those who taught modern languages, either as a social accomplishment or for commerce, and mathematics, either for commerce or for the emergent professions such as land surveyor and navigator.[4] On the other, lower still down the hierarchical scale, were those who ran private schools to provide teaching in the three Rs (the originators of the later dame schools). Quite different from all of these, in both status and function, were the graduate private tutors in the houses of the upper classes.[5]

A similarly hierarchical heterogeneity is to be found in the clerical profession ranging from those at the top of the tree, the scholar-theologians, the bishops, the deans and the archdeacons down to the parish priests, sometimes university graduates, sometimes illiterate. In the remoter areas were to be found the lectors or readers — men who, though not in holy orders, were empowered to read matins and evensong, to bury the dead, to read the homilies but not of course to administer the sacraments. These in their turn would themselves be distinguished from those graduate lecturers to be found in the larger towns and more particularly in London, who gave sermons during the weekdays in open places and were more often than not on the radical wing of the profession.

In the face of such diversity it would be foolhardy, if not impossible, to talk in general terms about the education of the professions. Such complexity of structure and function was obviously based on a wide range of professional preparation. It would seem, however, that a major factor in the development of a profession has been the degree to which its education has been institutionalized, and it is not surprising, therefore, that the traditional professions and those having the higher status are the graduate professions, i.e. those professions whose members have received their education at a university institution. But as soon as one tries to exemplify the generalization it begins to break down. For example, amongst the medicals the physicians required a university degree in medicine before they could be licensed by the College of Physicians, which had been founded in 1518. The surgeons on the other hand were not university-trained at all. They received their professional training through apprenticeship, were qualified by the Company of Barber Surgeons, and indeed did not break free of the Barbers until 1745. The apothecaries, perhaps the most important part of the profession when it came to treating the sick, were similarly apprenticed and qualified through their guild, the Company of Grocers, separating off in 1617 and forming their own Worshipful Company of Apothecaries, though not without some dissension within their own ranks, for the Grocers were a wealthy and prestigious company.[6]

The same kind of heterogeneity is to be found in the legal profession. The barristers received their professional education at the

Inns of Court, some, though by no means all, having spent time at university prior to being admitted to an Inn. Originally solicitors had also received their training at Inns of Court, but gradually during the sixteenth century they were forced out of the Inns of Court into their own Inns of Chancery and in the end became a non-graduate profession relying on the form of apprenticeship called serving articles which remains to this day.[7]

As for the teachers, the masters and ushers of grammar schools would be graduates (and indeed would often attempt to assert their superior status over other teachers by refusing to teach the so-called petties in the rudiments of their own language). Having received a university education, however, the grammar school teachers had then to seek a licence to teach from the Church. Academically qualified by the university's award of a degree they were professionally qualified by the bishop of the diocese in which they wished to teach, the criterion of adequacy or competence being whether the person concerned was a member of the established church who was willing to help rear the flock of that church. And this professional licensing by the bishop was backed up (with varying degrees of efficiency) through visitations and appearance before the archdeacon's court for those who defaulted. It should be remembered, however, that though licences to teach were issued in some cases 'to teach grammar', in others the teacher's function was limited 'to teach to read, write and cast accounts'. Not all graduates received the first category of licence, though a majority did. What is remarkable is the number of graduates who received the other kind of licence.[8] Of the clerics I want to say something later. Suffice it to say here that throughout the sixteenth century there was an increasing tendency for the ordinary parish priest to be a graduate. At the beginning of the century the majority were not graduates, but at the end the majority were. Like the teachers they received no direct professional preparation for their work. Many, in fact, combined the work of teaching with that of a curacy. Indeed some graduates took to teaching until a preferment came their way. The distinctions between the two professions were often decidedly imprecise.

But perhaps we are making our criteria too formal. It could be argued of the teachers, for example, that their claim to professional status (if not social status) rested not on formal qualifications but on the evidence we have of their professional interest in their work, their willingness to debate matters of professional concern, their awareness of the importance of their professional work. There is ample evidence in the sixteenth century of teachers' concern as to whether children should be taught in the 'common' schools or by private tutors, as to what were the virtues and weaknesses of a common style of teaching. Equally discussed as matters of professional concern were such topics as the role of the parent in the child's education, attitudes to corporal punishment, the role of the vernacular in education, the need to take account of differential learning skills, the need for maintaining standards in the profession. These matters were not, of course, debated in an organized way through the medium of a professional association. But the concern is there nevertheless, expressed in the professional manual treatises written by professional educators who were concerned with professional standards. More important, perhaps, we find evidence of the debate not only in the works of the famous grammar school masters, but also in books written for those lower down the professional scale. Take for example Francis Clement's *The Petie Schole* (1576), written for those teaching the elements outside the grammar schools. On behalf of these members of the profession he wrote 'I covet an end of all ignorant teaching'.[9] Similarly, Edmund Coote's *The English Schoolmaster* (1596) was written expressly 'for men and women of trade as tailors, weavers, shopkeepers, seamstresses and others' who would take on the elementary education of children. One index of the importance of books such as this is the fact that in 1737 *The English Schoolmaster* was published in its 54th edition.

I have referred to status several times. The historian of education is interested in this aspect of the matter in so far as education contributes to social status of particular professions and of particular groups within a profession. In addition, of course, he is interested in the social status of the wide range of practitioners making up the teaching profession. A relatively common feature of the upper echelons of the professions was their insistence that status derives not from professional skill but from general education. The medical profession have for long shown this insistence. For example, a fourteenth-century medical writer on surgery, Guy de Chauliac, insisted that 'if the doctors have not learnt geometry, astronomy, dialectics, or any other good discipline soon the leatherworkers, carpenters and furriers will quit their own occupations and become doctors'[10] (and we can recognize his list of disciplines as an incomplete summary of the seven liberal arts). This was exactly what Derwent Coleridge aimed to do with his training college students in the nineteenth century, and of course was roundly condemned for encouraging them to have aspirations above their station.

But this leads us to a paradox. Any study of the professions and their education must take account of the anti-intellectual side of a debate which was latent in the sixteenth century, explicit and virulent in the early seventeenth century, and which related to the clerical profession. No other profession was faced with this paradoxical situation which rested on a fundamental question, namely, was it *necessary* for a priest to be educated (in the formal sense) to fulfil his prime function? The varied answers, indeed the diametrically opposed answers, given to this question arose, not surprisingly, from a difference of opinion about the answer to another prior question, what is the prime function of a priest? There was no one agreed answer to this, and there were indeed major differences of opinion within the Protestant faith, even within the Puritan ranks. If the function of a priest was to go through a pre-ordained ritual laid down in the Prayer Book and to read a chosen piece from the Book of Homilies then obviously he had no need for a higher education. If his main function, however, was preaching, and in particular preparing his own sermons rather than reading a homily, and interpreting rather than reading scriptures, then a learned clergy was essential. The paradox lies, however, in the fact that though many of the sectaries shared this emphasis on a preaching clergy, they insisted that provided the priest was imbued with God's grace and the Holy Spirit then this was enough. No amount of human learning would make up for a lack of grace and spirit, and indeed the trappings of learning would be a possible hindrance, for they would intrude between priest and parishioner, as, so the sectaries argued, they most obviously and dangerously did between the Anglican priests and their flock. If God's word was swaddled in a cloak of learning how could the flock possibly take on the responsibility for their own spiritual salvation?[11]

When Anglicans like Laud argued on behalf of a learned ministry they were accused by the sectaries of merely wishing to maintain a buffer between the priest and his flock, which was much more a political and social than a religious matter, the maintenance of a social hierarchy and of the priest's place in the upper part of that hierarchy. Hence their attack not only on learning as such but on the institutions providing that learning, the universities, filled as they were with dissolute dons corrupting their willing students with the example of their own life-style, emphasizing hierarchy by their distinctions of academic dress, academic degrees, academic ritual and ceremony, basing their teaching on pagan philosophy, and even putting forward the

C

heathenistic notión of learning for the pleasure of learning. The railing-off of the Communion Table and the wearing of the surplice and other ecclesiastical vestments were seen to be merely further manifestations of a move away from the pure Christianity of the simple, unlearned fishermen and craftsmen who were Jesus' disciples. You will remember that John Brinsley, the author of *Ludus Literarius* and *A Consolacion for our Grammar Schooles*, curate of the parish and master of Ashby de la Zouch grammar school, was deprived of his post by the bishop of Lincoln in 1604 for refusing to wear the surplice, and ultimately lost his diocesan licence to teach.

Heterogeneity, then, was a marked characteristic of the professions in the sixteenth century, with differences between as well as within the groupings. If one can make any generalization about them it is that they were becoming increasingly aware of the social justification for their professionalization, looking upon the social problems of the day and reckoning that they could be overcome by the educated professional. Ignorance, and the social evils which arose from it, were seen not simply as a matter of God's moving in a mysterious way, but something which in part at least was man-made, and therefore in some degree eradicable by men. In particular it would be eradicated by the trained professional, whose willingness to subject traditional notions about ends and means, about roles and assumptions, to professional scrutiny distinguished his profession from that of a craft.[1][2]

Notes

1   On the profession of architect, for example, see N. Pevsner, 'The term "architect" in the Middle Ages', *Speculum*, XVII (1942), pp.549−62; L. F. Salzman, *Building in England down to 1540* (Oxford, Clarendon Press, 1952); H. M. Colvin (ed.), *The History of the King's Works*, 2 vols (London, H.M.S.O., 1963); L. R. Shelby, *John Rogers, Tudor Military Engineer* (i.e. surveyor of works) (Oxford, Clarendon Press, 1967).
2   F. D. Maurice, *Has the Church or the State the Power to Educate the Nation? A Course of Lectures* (1839), pp.188−9.
3   *Report of H. M. Commissioners on the State, Discipline, Studies and Revenues of the University and Colleges of Oxford*, p.94, B.P.P. 1852 [1482] xxii.
4   Cf. Kenneth Charlton, *Education in Renaissance England* (London, Routledge and Kegan Paul, 1965), Ch. IX; 'The teaching profession in sixteenth and seventeenth century England', in P. Nash (ed.), *History and Education: The Educational Uses of the Past* (New York, 1970) pp.24−61.

5   A detailed study of private tutors still remains to be done. The local history of the schoolteaching profession is being undertaken by Dr Rosemary O'Day, Mr C. D. Rogers and Mr J. P. K. Orpen. Cf. Margaret Spufford, 'The schooling of the peasantry in Cambridgeshire 1575–1700', *Agricultural History Review*, 18 (1970), Supplement, pp.122–47, especially pp.123 ff.

6   For the relations between the Royal College of Physicians and the barber surgeons, apothecaries and midwives, cf. Sir Geoffrey L. Keynes, *Life of William Harvey* (Oxford, Clarendon Press, 1966), Chs.6, 8 and 26; Sir George Clark, *A History of the Royal College of Physicians*, I (Oxford, Clarendon Press, 1964); C. Wall (revised by E. A. Underwood), *A History of the Worshipful Company of Apothecaries*, I (London, Wellcome Historical Medical Museum, 1963); W. S. C. Copeman, *The Worshipful Company of Apothecaries of London: A History 1617–1967* (Oxford, Pergamon Press, 1967).

7   For the barristers, cf. W. R. Prest, *The Inns of Court* (London, Longman, 1972); for the solicitors, Michael Birks, *Gentleman of the Law*, (London, Stevens, 1960).

8   Cf. W. E. Tate, 'The episcopal licensing of teachers in England', *Church Quarterly Review*, CLVII (4) (1956), pp.426–32; S. M. Wide and J. A. Morris, 'The episcopal licensing of schoolmasters within the Diocese of London', *Guildhall Miscellany*, II (1960–8), pp.392–406; W. H. Frere (ed.), *Visitation Articles and Injunctions of the Period of the Reformation* (London, Alcuin Club Collections, 1910); W. P. M. Kennedy (ed.), *Elizabethan Episcopal Administration*, 3 vols (London, Mowbray, 1924).

9   Francis Clement, *The Petie Schole with an English Orthographie.* Though first published in 1576 the earliest extant edition is dated 1587. The text is reprinted in R. D. Pepper (ed.), *Four Tudor Books on Education* (Gainesville, Florida, 1966).

10   Cited V. L. Bullough, 'Education and professionalization: an historical example', *History of Education Quarterly*, X (2) (1970), pp.60–9.

11   Cf. H. Schultz, *Milton and Forbidden Knowledge* (New York, 1955).

12   For the social and patriotic awareness of that emergent professional, the writer, cf. E. Miller, *The Professional Writer in Elizabethan England* (Cambridge, Mass., 1959).

T. W. BAMFORD

Public School Masters:
A Nineteenth–Century Profession

When, in 1861, a Royal Commission was appointed 'to inquire into the Revenues and Management of Certain Colleges and Schools, and the studies pursued and the instruction given therein', it dealt with nine schools. Two of these were day schools, St Paul's and Merchant Taylors', the other seven were boarding schools, Eton, Winchester, Westminster, Charterhouse, Harrow, Rugby and Shrewsbury. This selection gave a certain standing to this group of schools. At the opening of the nineteenth century, however, of the seven boarding schools, only Eton's position was secure. Winchester had a certain reputation and Westminster was in decline. The rest that were of any significance were few in number: Harrow was well known, Shrewsbury and Charterhouse can only be included with grave misgivings, and then of course there was the new upstart of Rugby. Each member of this second group of three or four was small in size and subject to alarming variations in intake. At the end of the century this initial group of seven had swollen to forty or so, large by the standards of their time and, what is more important, stable.

Public schools employed many kinds of staff, but the only ones of a status that mattered were the masters. Teachers of modern languages were often called 'extra masters', and confusion may arise at some schools as a result, particularly at the end of the century, but numbers were few. The rest of the staff had comparatively little status and responsibility in decision-making.

If we consider appointments in the nineteenth century at four boarding schools (Eton, Harrow, Shrewsbury, Rugby) and one day school (St Paul's) we find that half had fathers from the professional class (for details see Table 1): 30 per cent of all fathers were churchmen, and another 20 per cent were the sons of adminstrators and

29

Table 1. *Teachers in public schools and parental status in the nineteenth century*

Eton appointments: 1800–1861

Others: 1800–1899

Status of father	No. of school teachers employed at						Percentage of school teachers employed at					
	Eton	Harrow	Shrewsbury	Rugby	St Paul's	Total 5 Schools	Eton	Harrow	Shrewsbury	Rugby	St Paul's	All 5 Schools
Titled, gentry, men of property, etc.	9	20	7	23	13	72	10	18	10	18	16	14
Professional class: Administration — Governmental, Empire, regional, officers of armed forces	5	6	4	5	1	21	6	6	6	4	1	5
Churchmen	34	26	25	41	16	142	38	24	36	32	20	30
Scholastic: university and headmasters and assistants in grammar and public schools	5	15	3	10	7	40	6	14	4	8	9	8
The law, medicine and other professions	7	6	5	6	7	31	8	6	7	5	9	7
Middle and lower classes	9	9	9	7	8	42	10	8	13	6	10	9
Overseas	0	6	3	2	6	17	0	6	4	2	8	4
Unknown parental background	20	20	14	33	22	109	22	18	19	26	28	23
Totals	89	108	70	127	80	474						

officials, scholastics, the law, medicine and other professions. Of the rest, 14 per cent came from the gentry-titled-rich bracket while in 23 per cent of cases information was insufficient to form any judgement on parental background. It is likely that many of these unknowns came from the lower and middle classes and would thus swell the 9 per cent known to come from this group. The masters therefore came from all sections of society, with the professional background well represented. Although there were variations between the five schools, the social cross-section was astonishingly uniform. Thus at every school the largest single category was churchmen and the proportion of middle and lower class backgrounds only varied between 6 and 13 per cent. This is rather surprising for schools as widely different as Eton and St Paul's. Preliminary work on Clifton and Cheltenham would indicate a similar pattern there. The romantic idea that public school teaching was a significant avenue for the upward mobility of poor boys is not supported by the facts, at least at the main schools.

Although parental background was of importance in the nineteenth century, other factors influenced status, such as educational background and salary.

The school education of public school masters varied from school to school. Three-quarters (74 per cent) of Etonian masters were old Etonians. This is exceptional; the proportion of old boys on the staff was far less at other schools. The corresponding figures for Rugby and Shrewsbury were 28 and 27 per cent respectively. In general, the less famous or socially significant the school the fewer the masters who had been educated at the seven leading boarding schools. Indeed at St Paul's, one of the leading day schools, masters came in roughly equal numbers from the seven, from other public schools and from grammar schools.[1] It is, however, at university level that the real significance of the education of the masters is seen.

If we take the same five schools already considered, then out of 474 appointments in the nineteenth century, 453 had been educated at Oxford or Cambridge. Of the balance of 21, 15 were graduates of some foreign university, usually employed for modern language work. As stated earlier, not all the schools included such exceptions as true members of staff.

The situation seen in these five schools is typical of the rest, and for all practical purposes, masters in all public schools were restricted to Oxford and Cambridge products. The typical master was therefore a product of one of the seven boarding schools and an Oxbridge graduate.

Socially he came from a professional background, preferably with his father in the Church. Apart from the university connection, the less significant the school the more were these criteria relaxed. Vacancies were rarely advertised; selections were made either from men the heads knew personally as old boys, or from the grapevine with the colleges of the two universities. A former headmaster translated to the headship of a college could also be a potent source of information. Evidence for these methods arises from the correspondence and journeys of men such as Samuel Butler, Arnold, Temple, Benson, Vaughan, Wilson, H.M. Butler and Percival.

The schools were, in many ways, a deliberate extension of Oxford and Cambridge into the lower age range, so that boys moved out from school into the similar environment of the university and met it again on returning as assistant masters. The result was a tightly knit profession with common ideals. Allegiance to Oxford and Cambridge was seen in every phase of life: the classical culture, ceremonies, architecture, gowns, sport, religion, chapel ritual, meals in halls. But for the masters, it was a very narrow experience indeed. They knew little of the outside world and they lived in isolated communities which made them narrower still as they grew older. It is not surprising that so many developed eccentricities.

The ultimate goal of school life was university entrance and university mystique, in spite of the fact that the usual proportion of boys going to the university was between 35 and 40 per cent in the main schools (much less for those on the fringe).[2] In one sense it could be said that the majority were being sacrificed for the sake of the minority, although a great deal depends on whether such goals are considered as desirable educational ends in their own right apart from their university fulfilment.[3]

The schools went to extraordinary lengths to get their boys to Oxford and Cambridge, particularly by the provision of scholarships. Such awards were given both by the colleges and the schools, and it was calculated that, at the very beginning of twentieth century (1901), there were nearly 800 scholarships and exhibitions at Oxford of a value varying from £20 or less to £100 p.a.[4] The attractiveness and publicity value of these for the schools led to a concentration on a few subjects for each boy and a very high standard of achievement (degree standards in the opinion of many critics). To do well they required boys of high calibre, and the competition between the colleges and between the schools to get the best brains was an outstanding feature of the late nineteenth-century scene. The consistent winning of scholarships gave the schools great prestige and added to the professional status of the masters, but it also had financial implications. In the words of E. Lyttleton in 1900:

> During the last thirty or forty years the system of entrance scholarships has been enormously extended among the Public Schools. It was found that the large endowments of Eton and Winchester were attracting the very pick of the cleverest boys . . . it was natural that other schools which had risen in importance since the middle of the century should do their best to draw some supplies from the same source; that is, to hold out prospects of gratuitous or nearly gratuitous education to the clever sons of impecunious parents. . . . about 1885 every school of any prominence at all, and many grammar schools that could ill afford it, were offering substantial reductions to boys – even the large foundations, such as Marlborough, Repton, Haileybury, Clifton, Rossall and others, thought it necessary to institute or augment scholarships in order to prevent the absorption of all the rising talent by the other foundations.[5]

Success went to the schools with the best financial and business methods. In this way the supply of clever boys became unevenly distributed and formed a 'conglomeration in three or four of the best known public schools'.[6]

The possibility of using the scholarship system for educational ends was well understood. Thus, in the 1860s, J.M. Wilson wrote:

> If the colleges, for example, ceased to demand Latin verses for their scholarships; Latin verse would almost die before the breath of their disfavour. If the colleges offered scholarships and exhibitions, to acknowledge and encourage the study of science at schools, then the teaching of science would at once be naturalized in most of the schools which contribute many men to the universities.[7]

As part of these developments, the numbers and costs of these scholarships at the schools rose steadily. In 1880 it was calculated that £87,000 was spent by about 40 public boarding schools and this rose to £100,000 in 1893. All this sounds impressive and laudable but it had a disastrous effect upon the assistant staff. As W.H.D. Rouse put it in 1903:

> With richly endowed schools, where masters are fairly paid, this

expenditure (on scholarships) is not so hardly felt, though even there, other things (such as educational plant) are sadly wanting, and the school buildings are often unhealthy and inconvenient. But what shall we say of schools with no endowment, such as Clifton and Cheltenham, or schools like Bedford, which takes advantage of its endowment to lower the school fees? In all these the masters' salaries are low, often disgracefully low; and it ought to be the first care of a Governing Body that the staff is paid as generously as can be done, before offering money as bait for clever boys. Open scholarships in most schools are practically given at the masters' cost.[8]

It was a circular and socially self-defeating situation. The sons of well-to-do parents got the scholarships because the parents could afford special tuition in preparatory schools and at public schools to the exclusion of poor boys.

Altogether it would seem that the preparatory schools, public schools and universities were bound together educationally. Increasingly, in the second and third quarters of the nineteenth century and beyond, prestige was reckoned in terms of scholastic results, which in turn were synonymous with the winning of open scholarships to Oxford and Cambridge. This was linked with publicity and the success of the schools. The public schools were in the middle and were forced to fight for the limited talent available by offering scholarships. Unless the school was well endowed, these and other prestige items, like chapels and similar showpieces, could only be paid for out of the salaries of the masters. The scholarship system of the universities therefore had the effect of drastically lowering the standard of living of their own graduates. Oxbridge, therefore, gave its sons professional status in one way but helped to deny them the fruits of it.

The influence was not entirely one way. The increasing intimacy of the schools and the university had its effect as the century progressed. Indeed, Pattison complained that Jowett had turned the university away from higher research and learning to being a super public school. That the schools possessed both influence and the solidity of an established organization was one of the bases of any claim to professionalism on the part of the schools, as partners in the joint enterprise of educating the nation's talent.

On general grounds one would expect the salaries of public school masters to vary greatly, and the details given for the period around 1863 in Table 2 support this view. If we take Harrow as an example,

Table 2. Selected salaries in education 1860–65

H Harrow
R Rugby
W Westminster
S Shrewsbury
C Charterhouse
MT Merchant Taylors'
SP St Paul's
A All assistant staff
* Headmaster
[1] Rare and usually with profits from boarders
[2] Often run as a business or a family concern

Public schools / Other schools

Salary range in £ p.a.	H	R	W	S	C	MT	SP	Minor & new public schools	Preparatory schools	Grammar schools	Private academies	Elementary schools	Workhouse
5000–5999	*												
4000–4999													
3500–3999													
3000–3499		*											
2500–2999													
2000–2499				*									
1500–1999	6	4											
1000–1499	3	2	*	1	*	*	*			*[1]			
500–999	5	8	3	4	1	1	1	*	*				
0–499	2	2	4	4	4	4	3	A	A	A	A*[2]	A*	A*

35

then the headmaster earned £6,288 per year, but since it was claimed that he usually contributed to new buildings and improvements, then a figure in excess of £5,000 would seem reasonable. Six men received salaries between £1,500 and £1,999 p.a., three between £1,000 and £1,499 and five between £500 and £999. The housemaster was the lucrative post, and such posts went usually by seniority, so that an income in excess of £1,500 was within the expectation of any member of staff if he stayed long enough. A similar situation existed at Eton and Rugby. In addition there were many perks, particularly at Eton, such as free housing, private coaching, curacies and the prospect of a rectorship (virtually certain at Eton if desired) for retirement, if not before. Of the other Clarendon schools, Winchester was lower than the Harrow-Rugby standard, and the others in salary order would be Shrewsbury, Westminster, Charterhouse, Merchant Taylors', St Paul's. At St Paul's the High Master's income was £900 with free residence, gown and the rent of two houses; three classical masters' income lay between £300 and £400 with free residence and gown in each case. Three other masters received between £100 and £200 without the extras and were responsible for mathematics and French.[9] The sharp distinction between classical masters and others was usual, with the exception of the 'big' schools.

A few grammar schools approximated to the position of St Paul's, as did a few of the new boarding schools, but in general assistant masters were lucky to get £100–200 p.a. These figures should be compared with a lower-class wage range of £34–71 at the same period.[10]

The position in the 1860s persisted till the end of the century with a tendency to a levelling out of the differences. The lower-class wage rose by some 40 per cent and the salary of the elementary school teachers doubled (although this varied geographically and at different levels). As for grammar schools, the salary of assistants, usually graduates, varied from £50 to £300 p.a. according to school and grade. In general, a man was fortunate to earn more than £120.[11] In public schools the gap between the headmaster and the rest remained, and the remuneration of an assistant at the three main schools (Eton, Harrow and Rugby) continued to be above that of headmasters elsewhere. The discrepancy over almost the entire range of public schools remained one of the major abuses of the nineteenth century. In theory the responsibility lay with the trustees in each case, but the fact that not one of them did anything to solve the problem shows how far they had relinquished their powers. In fact the responsibility for the pitifully low salaries in most cases was due to the rapaciousness of headmasters, for they themselves saw that the others suffered financially from the important and expensive exercise of bolstering school prestige.

The style of living of public school masters can be deduced in part from the factual details of the successive census returns, and in part from newspapers, correspondence, memoirs and novels.

Even allowing for the complication of boarders, the assistant classical staff at two of the main schools at least (Harrow and Rugby) lived in very comfortable and spacious houses (some of which still exist) with at least two servants. With a small family of young children, there would be a nursemaid as well, sometimes two. These menials lived in and were on constant call; other servants were employed on a day basis. This applied at least for the second half of the century.

With a boarding house the master was even better placed with extra staff and facilities which could be utilized by his own household as the need arose. The economics of mass catering were also used for preferential treatment in the local shops and for even greater economies (and personal wealth) in the era of the mass distribution of stores from London later in the century. It was argued that this gracious living was desirable and even necessary since wealthy and important parents paid visits to their sons, especially at times of sickness, and the social reputation of the school was at stake. At other schools with less salary and less significant connections, the spaciousness and the help would be cut down accordingly.

The headmasters of the 'three' (Eton, Harrow and Rugby) dwelt in even more spacious houses provided by the school. Goulburn of Rugby, who lived with his wife and mother-in-law (and no children), had eight servants seeing to the household, transport and garden duties; and this number was for his own immediate needs — another set of servants was involved in the boarding house. All these servants lived in; there were undoubtedly 'dailies' in addition. If we compare this with other houses then the *ménage* of these top headmasters indicates a style approaching that of minor gentry. In some other ways they also acquired habits which may be broadly termed 'gentry': the urge to travel; the acquisition of another (country) house, so that they could spend part of the year away and indulge in a kind of seasonal migration; the collection of items of culture from libraries to old master paintings.

The facts concerning the earning power of the staff may possibly have led to the assumption that the more efficient and luckier teachers would become headmasters in turn. This is not necessarily true.

From 1800 to 1900, there were in all seven appointments to Harrow as headmaster, and, of these, five had had no experience of schools at all and even the other two (Welldon and Wood) had been appointed previously, without experience, to the headmastership of another school lower in the hierarchy. In terms of fact, therefore, the headmaster's chair at Harrow was totally inaccessible to the ranks of any school. In other words, there was no point in joining the staff at any school anywhere in the hope of becoming headmaster of Harrow. The opposite case is Eton. There, all seven heads appointed in the century were appointed from the masters of Eton. In this case it was impossible for anyone outside the staff to be elected, so that anyone outside Eton staff had no chance of entering that particular élite. At Rugby, seven of the nine cases were recruited either from the university direct (one case), or from other posts outside the schools (four), or from headmasters of other schools who had had no assistant master experience (two).

In general, it may be said that as the century went on, more appointments were made from men with experience in the schools and that this was particularly so of the new schools. Thus all five Marlborough appointments went to experienced men. Sometimes schools were linked with colleges at Oxford and Cambridge, and when this was the case, as at Merchant Taylors' (three cases out of three) and Sedbergh (three out of five), the headships went to men straight from the university. The procedure may appear to lack system, but it must be remembered that these were top jobs with very high rewards if only in terms of salary. The scramble to get them was correspondingly fierce.

If we ignore the case of Eton, then headmasters at top schools in the nineteenth century were chosen either (even preferably) from men outside the profession altogether or from those holding the following posts:

> headmasters of: Dulwich, Tonbridge, Midhurst, Bradfield, Cheltenham (2), Kensington G.S., Christ's Hospital.
> assistant masters of: Rugby, Harrow.

Of this list, Midhurst concerned an appointment made in 1806 and the appointment from the headship of Kensington G.S. was the first headmaster of Marlborough.

Heads were chosen from specified routes, either from well-connected young men with no experience at all, from the assistants of a top school or the heads of reputable public schools somewhat lower in the hierarchy. If the gulf between the previous post and the new appointment was too great, then trouble ensued, as in the case of Hayman at Rugby in the 1870s.

The fact of selection from the large number of well-qualified contestants would indicate that, in the choice of headmasters, certain channels of influence were important and affected the trustees who made the appointments.

One of the influential channels was the significant headmaster. It is well-known, for example, that Frederick Temple of Rugby possessed a talent for creating headmasters. What is really meant is that compared with other headmasters his word and recommendations were accepted in preference to those of other headmasters by key men among the selecting bodies. He had already been a prominent man in the central administration before going to Rugby, and his advice on educational matters, including where appropriate the appointment of headmasters, was sought by such men as Gladstone, Lingen, Forster and the Prince Consort. One can trace at least five of the appointments to the major schools mentioned earlier directly to his influence (not just the writing of testimonials), and he certainly had a hand in several others. Altogether Temple is the outstanding case in the middle and later nineteenth century, with Arnold a celebrated case earlier on. The fact that these men of influence and so many others were connected with the intellectual aristocracy is no coincidence either. Arnold, the two Vaughans (C.J. and W.W.), the Butlers (G.(two), A.G., H.M. and S.), G. Moberly, the Temples (F. and W.), Benson, Wickham, J.M. Wilson, G.G. Bradley and J. Robertson were members of this intellectual club. In a similar way many headmasters had powerful friends, powerful enough to account for their election through the trustee network before appointment. These include the three Butlers (H.M., G. and G.), G. Cotton, F.W. Farrar, Prince Lee, J. Percival and A.C. Tait. Again, many had famous teachers. Naturally, it was safer for the applicant to possess more than one of these advantages if possible. This does not, of course, mean that anyone without connections at birth could not become a headmaster, but it does mean that such a person had to forge his connections early on and that he would be in competition with others with wider connections. It follows that such people were rare in the second half of the century although a few examples may be quoted. The nature, variety and significance of such underlying influence raises many problems – moral as well as educational and functional. It is a poignant fact that any person without connections who entered public school as a teacher with the hope of becoming a significant headmaster some day was doomed to disappointment.

The headmasters already mentioned were important people in education, but how did they rate among other leaders of English society? Some indication may be gained by the interchangeability of jobs at this top level. J. Percival passed from Clifton to the headship of an Oxford college, to Rugby and on to a bishopric direct. H.A. James went from the headship of Rossall to a deanery and then to headmasterships at Cheltenham and Rugby before going to Oxford as head of a college. It is clear that the headmastership of Rugby was not inferior to a deanery or the headship of an Oxford college. The difference between these jobs lay in their psychological attraction, not their status.

At Harrow, out of seven heads who retired in the nineteenth century, four went directly to high office in the Church, one becoming a canon, one a dean and two becoming bishops. In addition Charles Vaughan accepted a bishopric and then withdrew his acceptance though he was later made a dean. Another, George Butler, became a dean some years after he left Harrow while Joseph Drury, after some years of retirement in the country, was given a prebend in Wells Cathedral. At Rugby, out of nine heads who retired in the nineteenth century the two first merely retired while the rest produced the sad case of Hayman, two bishops, three deans and Arnold. These posts were often stepping stones and from the combined Harrow-Rugby contingent of headmasters were produced no less than three archbishops of Canterbury — Longley, Tait and Frederick Temple (not to mention other archbishops including Benson from the ranks of the assistants).

The record of these two schools (Rugby and Harrow) is quite outstanding. By tradition a man could expect a deanery at least. All this confirms the financial conclusions that the headmasters of these schools formed an educational summit — an élite, in fact, if we define an élite as a small section of society which has recognized power and influence and is apt to be asked for advice by the Government and to receive major honours in return. It also means that, in the eyes of some men at least, several jobs were regarded as roughly equivalent: headmaster of the three major schools, dean or bishop in the Church, head of an Oxford or Cambridge college. Of course, one has reservations. Thus there are grades in deaneries and there is a world of difference between the Master of Trinity (although H.M. Butler went to Trinity from Harrow) and the heads of some other colleges. Nevertheless the evidence is clear, and emphasizes once again the close connection between the public schools and the Church on the one hand and the public schools and universities on the other.

The fact is, however ridiculous it may seem to us now, that some of the schools in the last half of the century were equivalent, if not superior, to some of the Oxford colleges. When Percival was President of Trinity, Oxford, and was offered the headship of Rugby, an Oxford colleague expressed it like this: ' . . . but the position of Head of Rugby is probably one of the most important in England, and it would have been a folly, I think, if you had rejected it.[12]

Nevertheless, there is a distinctive difference between a school and a university, if only because it means movement from quiet contemplation to the battlefield. It may well be asked, therefore: what makes a man move to a school in this way? the answer is power. The headmaster was a potentate and there was no other job quite like it. Percival once said: 'Oxford had as much feeling of unity as a rabbit warren; each head of college was seen at the mouth of his burrow; but if anything is suggested in he dived.'[13]

At a school, when the headmaster appeared it was everyone else who dived out of sight.

The same kind of career can be seen in some other schools. Winchester and Shrewsbury and also some (three or four) newer ones, Marlborough, Wellington and, rather lower, Cheltenham and Clifton. Thus of three successive masters of Marlborough (Cotton, Bradley and Farrar) one became a bishop direct and two became deans. By analogy, therefore, if deans and bishops comprise an élite group within the Church, then these select headmasterships also comprise an élite group. Appointment to the headmaster's chair of these nine schools – Eton, Harrow, Rugby, Winchester, Shrewsbury, Marlborough, Wellington, Cheltenham and Clifton – was more than just an educational niche but rather the creation of a man as heir apparent to a post of wider significance. The school was in fact merely a stepping stone in the man's career.

One might raise the question of the origin of this well-established élite existing at the end of the nineteenth century. The first two normal instances of headmasterly promotion (outside Eton and Westminster) were Samuel Butler of Shrewsbury and Longley of Harrow, while Arnold was on the verge of preferment about the same time. What precisely made this period of the 1830s so suitable for such a development is obscure. It was, of course, a period of great social and

D

religious unrest. The two were not unconnected, and the effort to resolve these problems and their potential connection with education may have been a contributing factor. There was also a new political atmosphere, and perhaps this made a new approach desirable. All this, however, is speculation, and illumination of this difficult problem must await further work.

One might well ask also why this élite group was restricted to a small number of schools? Did the large salaries attract the best people – the traditional explanation – or did the superior social position of the children mean that the headmasters became well known to the most influential parents in the land? A glance at the relative distribution of the children and their parents is enough to realize the potential of such an argument.

Again, there is the even more difficult problem of the relationship of ability, birth and influence. It has been mentioned that many influential people, including the important headmasters, are linked and that their linkage continues through time, giving its more able products a destiny, as it were. Indeed, as with royalty, the elevation of its more able members can be interpreted as one of its essential functions. Certainly if this did not happen it would soon cease to be an 'intellectual aristocracy' at all.

It would be easy to dismiss this conclusion as another of the unpleasant facts of the nineteenth century but the nature of this apex of the profession is far more complicated. The fact is that many of these men did in fact become outstanding members of Victorian society and it may be that such relationships produce, in some way difficult to understand, the requisite qualities that do not occur in more orthodox acceptable ways (or, as we might say, through sheer personal ability). This difficult but important problem must await research, but the same phenomenon is seen in such an intellectual and unlikely field as the winning of Nobel prizes. This is seen in a study of the relationships of English Nobel prizewinners, the statements of Sir Hans Krebs himself and the work on American prizewinners by Harriet Zuckerman.[14] All these revelations would indicate (together with a kinship in many English winners) that there is a relationship between influence and ability in a field where one would normally assume that isolated individual merit was paramount. In other words, the isolated worker is unlikely to win such prizes. There are, indeed, a few well-known central figures in science who somehow have the ability to create Nobel winners. Such relationships are a matter of fact, and may be due to the seminal figure inspiring the critical faculties of protégés to new and hitherto unsuspected heights. In the words of Krebs: '...in many instances, distinction breeds distinction or, in other words, distinction develops if nurtured by distinction.'[15]

In our own case, the question might well be asked: did some of the influential headmasters sit at the feet of kingmakers in their formative years as the scientists did, so that the example of the great men before them forced them to raise their critical sights, and spurred them to a greater effort? We do not know, but this certainly happened to the greatest headmaster of the nineteenth century (Arnold) and to Kennedy as well. Others could well be added since they were already born into an atmosphere of distinction.

During the nineteenth century, the number of public school boy boarders (aged thirteen and over) grew from about 1,500 in 1800 to 10,000 in 1900. This reflects a corresponding growth in the number of masters who had three things in common: employment at a public school with all that implied, an intimate relationship with the boarders, and an Oxford or Cambridge degree. At a time when degrees were relatively rare, membership of the graduate club bestowed a distinctive quality, apart from the possession of the common culture emanating from the older universities. On the other hand, the public schools did not possess a monopoly for the employment of graduates. The Bryce Report[16] tells us that there were at least 352 Oxford and Cambridge graduate headmasters of secondary schools in England and Wales, and the total of graduates employed in these schools would certainly have been several times that figure.

Although all public school masters had certain features in common, enough has been established here to indicate that there were significant divisions in the profession which prevent a simple view. Indeed there appear to be four distinct categories: headmasters of the few significant schools forming an élite; assistant masters at the three or four 'top' schools; headmasters of other public schools; the rest. Some idea of the size of these groups at two different periods is given in Table 3.

The first group was exceptional. In one sense it comprised an élite, in another its members used the schools as stepping stones to other things. In every way an enormous gulf existed between them and the rest. This gulf was not only in terms of salary and power, but also in terms of quality of experience, since many of the appointments (at any rate until the last quarter) seem to indicate that educational expertise was not an essential part of the background.

Table 3. *Possible structure of the public school profession in the nineteenth century*

	1866	1900
Headmaster élite	6	10
Assistant staff at four 'main' schools	57	100
Headmaster at other schools	15	30
Other assistant staff	285	500
Totals	363	640

The second group, comprising the staff of four schools, were either living in luxury or had firm prospects of it. As the century progressed many became heir to headships elsewhere, even to the élite. Promotion was theirs if they wished provided they were prepared to suffer a substantial loss in salary. In many ways this select band of masters may be coupled with the headmasters of the other schools, and in these two, taken jointly, the heart of the profession lay. The number in these two categories was not great, increasing from about 75 in 1866 to 130 or so at the end of the century.

The last group consisted of the rest of the assistant staff. This is perhaps the most interesting group sociologically, although we know least about it. Any estimation of the size of this group meets formidable problems of definition but perhaps a reasonable estimate would show an increase from 285 in 1866 to 500 in 1900. The boys in their care had not the status of those in the leading schools, and this group was paid varying amounts from the merest subsistence level in some cases to £400 for the favoured few. Their life was also subservient and usually lacked the stability and freedom of the staff at the 'big' schools. A few might gain promotion or a boarding house.

Altogether the staff of the public schools was too varied to be described in any precise way as a professional group. There are obvious grounds for considering the most eminent members as too exclusive for inclusion and the lowest members as too near the level of subsistence without any real hope of attaining professional status. The masters of the three or four schools and the headmasters elsewhere came nearest to the concept of professionalism.

It is often claimed that the sign of a profession is an official structure and organization with an associated college establishing standards of professional entry, training and conditions of work. There was nothing of this kind for the nineteenth-century public school staffs. There was no organization, no college, no training. All there was was membership of an Oxford or Cambridge college, which conferred a necessary status and qualification, and the studies pursued at the university providing knowledge to be transmitted, however imperfectly, to their pupils. They were just a group of people with properties in common selected by isolated heads with, in general, a keen sense of standards if not an agreed sense of remuneration. Certainly any attempt to organize the staff was not in the interests of the headmasters and would have limited their power. It was ironic that this select body of independent men was forced to combine in the so-called Headmasters' Conference when the Government proposed a bill which included, among other things, examinations and diplomas for teachers. In a sense the creation of the Headmasters' Conference did two things. It denied the setting-up of certain standards that could well have been the beginning of the organization of teachers. It also created a superficial top-level association that to some extent obscured the real issues.

The nearest parallel to the select band of public school teachers lies in the staffs of the older universities. The relationship between the two was quite intimate, and in the last century, when the university is said to have neglected research, tolerated diverse standards and even aped the public schools,[17] the parallels were probably at their closest. Indeed one could make out a strong case based on the thesis that both sets of staff were equivalent. It is not possible to pursue this important matter at this stage but one obvious factor in such a comparison is the importance of solidarity and the fact that everyone at the university lives together. From the school point of view, the real problem was, and still is, geographic isolation. If, somehow, all the schools had been grouped together in two or three places only, with the boys being educated together (although in separate schools) in the manner of the colleges at Oxford and Cambridge, then the story would have been vastly different. It was rendered impossible by the geographical location of endowments and, as a result, isolation produced power and independence on the one hand, and on the other bred all those anomalies and injustices which were so obvious in the nineteenth century.

Other interesting parallels in professionalism arose in the public service in the H.M. Inspectorate of Schools and the administrative civil service. Both of these had links with the old universities and the public schools. Indeed it seems fitting that the dominance of Thomas Arnold in the school world should have been reflected in that of his son, Matthew, in the Inspectorate. Here again, the post was one of power with few qualifications demanded for entrance beyond that of public school background and Oxford and Cambridge culture. Similarly with the administrative civil service. Before the Northcote-Trevelyan reforms, the aspirant required the hand of influence for nomination, and even afterwards a public school background with a university education (preferably in the classics) was essential in practice. Like teaching and the Inspectorate there was no training and the job was learned by doing it. Hence the name for this kind of administrator as 'generalist' or 'cultured amateur'.

All four occupations – public school masters, university dons, the educational inspectorate and the administrative civil service – had certain features in common including education for entry and an attitude to training. Whereas now (1973) it might possibly be said that the administrators have at last cast off their traditions with Fulton, the same traditions are still strong in the public schools.

Notes

1   For details see T.W. Bamford, *Rise of the Public Schools* (London, Nelson, 1967), p.121.
2   Of Rugby, Harrow, Winchester, Shrewsbury, St Paul's, no school sent more than forty-five per cent. For Charterhouse in the last quarter of the century the percentage going to Oxbridge varied between twenty-seven (1873) and forty (1896).
3   A similar situation was seen in State grammar schools in the twentieth century when the schools were geared for the few who went on to the university.
4   G. Balfour, *The Educational Systems of Great Britain and Ireland*, 2nd ed. (Oxford, Clarendon Press, 1903), p.238.
5   E. Lyttleton, 'Entrance scholarships to public schools and their influence on preparatory schools', in *Special Reports on Educational Subjects*, Vol.6 (1900), pp.91–2, B.P.P.1900 [Cd.418] xxii, Pt II.
6   Ibid. p.94.
7   J.M. Wilson, 'On teaching natural science in schools', in F.W. Farrar (ed.), *Essays on a Liberal Education* (London, Macmillan, 1867), p.288.
8   W.H.D. Rouse, 'Competition for open scholarships', in the *Schoolmasters Year Book and Directory* (1903), Pt III, p.54. See also similar sentiments in C. Norwood and Hope, *The Higher Education of Boys in England* (London, Murray, 1909).

9   *Report of H.M. Commissioners appointed to inquire into the revenues and management of certain colleges and schools*, Vol. I, p.189, B.P.P.1864 [3288] xx.

10   A.L. Bowley, *Wages and Income Since 1860* (Cambridge, University Press, 1937).

11   See the ranges and other data given in *Royal Commission on Secondary Education* (Bryce Report), Vol.IV, pp.538 et seq., B.P.P.1895 [C.7862 – III] xivi.

12   W. Temple, *Life of Bishop Percival* (London, Macmillan, 1921), p.91.

13   Ibid. p.53.

14   M.A. Krebs, 'The making of a scientist', *Nature*, 215 (30 Sept.1967), pp.1441–5; H. Zuckerman, 'The sociology of the Nobel Prizes', *Scientific American* (Nov.1967), Vol.217, No.5, pp.25–33.

15   M.A. Krebs, op. cit. p.1442.

16   *Royal Commission on Secondary Education*, Vol.IV, pp.561, etc.

17   See p.32.

J. L. DOBSON

The Training Colleges and their Successors 1920-1970

In the last fifty years there have been three major inquiries into the education and training of teachers – those conducted by the 1923–5 Departmental Committee, the 1944 McNair Committee and the 1971–2 Lord James Committee. If we include the inquiry into higher education undertaken in 1961–3 by the Lord Robbins Committee and the unfinished investigation by the Select Committee of the House of Commons in 1969–70, then the total is five. The frequency of these re-examinations of teacher education is significant, for it is a symptom of the unease felt at all levels in the educational hierarchy about the preparation of teachers in England and Wales. This unease was justified, because until recently this country had never had a consistent policy for the education of its teachers. Schemes of a sort, based upon expediency not principle, were framed to meet the immediate needs of the school system. Intending teachers were given a specific training for the kind of job they were expected to do, and the system had no wider or more luminous horizons than that. Before 1944 the pre-McNair training colleges processed teachers for the elementary schools. The university departments trained graduates, some of whom went into the elementary schools and others in increasing number into the secondary schools. Between 1946 and 1951 the emergency training colleges turned out teachers after a one-year course in order to remedy a drastic shortage of staff. Thus the training of teachers constantly reflected the structure and state of the schools, and changes in teacher education followed obediently changes in the schools. The theory of cultural lag in education suggests that technological and economic changes have a much delayed effect upon the educational programmes of schools, and these changes react upon teacher education at one further remove.

49

Teacher education has indeed seemed narrow and conservative in the past, rarely finding its own initiative.

Within the last twenty years the changing needs of the common primary schools and the common or comprehensive secondary schools have increasingly required teachers who are professional and expert educators rather than job operatives. Reacting to these needs, those concerned with teacher education have in recent years been seeking a new formula for a proper professional education for teachers, one that will transcend the narrow, specific practicalities of the past. This accounts for the succession of inquiries and reports. The argument can be challenged, not least by those who would claim that what is needed in teachers is more practical skill and less theoretical knowledge and scholarship. But historically this view has had a limiting, even depressing, effect upon the status of teachers and training colleges.

A Departmental Committee was appointed in 1923 to review the arrangements for the training of teachers for the public elementary schools and to consider possible changes in the organization and financing of the existing system. Ominously, it was to have regard to 'the economy of public funds'.[1] The chairman of the committee was Viscount Burnham and its members included Dr Ernest Barker, Professor Helen Wodehouse and Dame Margaret Lloyd George, and it might have been expected that its report would have favoured the training colleges. Instead it proved a profound disappointment for the colleges, chiefly because the growing connection with the universities was diminished and the three-year course for teachers was rejected. This was a reversal of the liberal trends in the development of the colleges before 1920, and it is interesting to see how and why such a retreat took place at this time.

The elementary schools and the training of the teachers who served in them had long suffered from the twin traditions of poverty and cheapness on the one hand and makeshift arrangements on the other, which stultified the work of both schools and colleges. There was a reluctance on the part of Governments and the public at large to acknowledge that the State had a duty to provide a universal, free and sufficient system of elementary and secondary education for the mass of the people. In the decades before and after 1900 cohorts of pupils flooded into the elementary schools. The new Board of Education, established in 1899, was hard put to find enough teachers to man these schools and look after classes – for many of the Article 68 'additional' women teachers could do little more than this, since they had had no training of any kind. The Board was equally unprepared for the task of supplying teachers for the secondary schools, which developed as part of the national system after 1902. The central authority and the new local education authorities had no master plan for educational development, so that elementary schools, secondary schools and teacher supply were dealt with separately, and the expansion of each was regulated by *ad hoc* decisions and piecemeal advances. Incidentally, one result of this patchwork kind of enterprise was the almost total neglect of our technical education at this time.

This fragmented policy is seen most clearly in the arrangements for the training of teachers. Day training colleges had been set up in 1890 and afterwards in the provincial universities and university colleges (and at Cambridge), and they offered courses for both non-graduate and undergraduate students who intended to enter teaching. By 1899 they were producing one-fifth of the total annual supply of trained teachers, and in the early years of this century about two-thirds of their output of teachers entered the elementary schools. The local education authorities were encouraged to set up their own training colleges after 1904, when the Board of Education decided to recognize and assist colleges other than voluntary and day training colleges, and by 1914 there were twenty-two local education authority colleges in existence. In 1908 the Board ruled that up to half the number of places at voluntary colleges had to be open to those who did not subscribe to the denominational tenets of the college concerned but who wished to enter. The pupil-teacher system was supplemented by schemes for 'bursars' and later 'student teachers', who received a secondary education up to the age of seventeen at least and also had concurrent or deferred teaching practice in schools, before going on to a training college to complete their education. By 1914 forty per cent of students entering colleges were in this category. The student-teacher system was only a modest improvement upon the pupil-teacher scheme, which it eventually replaced, and it gradually declined in importance until its extinction in 1939.

The Board of Education strove simultaneously to increase the supply of trained graduate teachers for the new secondary schools, and in 1911 they offered universities and university colleges grants for a four-year course of combined study. In their first three years the students were to give their time to the study of academic subjects required for the degree and in the fourth year exclusively to professional training for teaching. This scheme was formally embodied in the Board's Regulations for the

Training of Teachers in 1918, and it has continued to be the standard form of training for graduates since then, having been slightly modified in 1951 and now made compulsory. In 1914 nine university departments and five separate colleges were recognized as eligible for grant in respect of training graduate teachers. But in addition the Board also recognized similarly four schools – three for the training of graduates in the teaching of special subjects and one, Rugby School, for general training in connection with the Cambridge department. In 1920 there were twenty-two institutions recognized by the Board for the training of secondary school teachers. Of these fifteen were university departments of education; five were women's training colleges; and two were secondary schools.[2] The use of secondary schools for training graduates was an abortive expedient, which never embraced more than a handful of schools, and it petered out in the 1920s. But the fact that the Board had recourse to such a device at all illustrates the lack of any integral plan for the training of teachers.

The day training colleges and newer local education authority colleges deserved much of the credit for whatever progress the training colleges had made towards a more liberal and elevated interpretation of their function before 1920. The voluntary residential colleges, insufficient in number and small in size, had a lot of ground to make up, if they were to achieve parity with the new model colleges, but the incentive to do so was strong. The Report of the Board of Education for 1912–1913 devoted a whole chapter to a historical survey of the training of teachers in England and Wales, in which a comparison was made between earlier conditions in the colleges and recent improvements.

> The life of a student in the past was certainly Spartan. College buildings were not insanitary, but the rooms provided for the students were often bare and uncomfortable and occasionally squalid. In many colleges the dietary was monotonous and the meals were not always well cooked or properly served. Disciplinary rules were sometimes many and irksome; the hours of work long. There was little opportunity for recreation, social intercourse, or even private reading, since few colleges had students' common rooms or libraries worthy of the name.[3]

This would have served as an apt description of some of the colleges even at the time this report was written. Although some progress had been made, conditions in many of the older colleges were still archaic

and austere. In February 1902 the visiting H.M.I. had reported on
Exeter Diocesan College for men as follows:

> There were 90 students in residence. Five of them were reading for
> examinations of the London University. There were no students in
> the third year.
>
> No changes in staff have occurred. The students are in good
> discipline and display general satisfactory skills in teaching. They
> also read and write creditably. They have the opportunity of
> learning something of horticulture under the Principal's direction in
> the College garden. I am glad to know that it is intended to open the
> new recreation room for use by the students in the autumn. I trust
> the Committee will soon be in a position to provide proper cubicles
> in the dormitories, in which they are needed, and to form the
> nucleus of a College library.[4]

In some places not much advance upon these standards had been
made by 1920. Many colleges still had a severely institutional air about
them, and the students knew no indulgence. Their days were fully
occupied, and the dreary round of instruction, private study and the
delivery of model and 'criticism' lessons had not altered appreciably in
twenty years. The opportunity for breaking out of this traditional
mould seemed to lie in the emulation of the day training colleges, the
improvement of academic standards, and the attraction of better
students by the offer of degree courses.

The example of the day training colleges had undoubtedly afforded
the prospect of emancipating growth for other colleges, which had
shared indirectly in their success. The day training colleges provided
two-year and three-year courses of study, and for their better students,
those judged capable of advanced work, these led to a university degree.
Their students sat side by side with other university students in the
same classes for their academic studies. The residential colleges also had
two-year and three-year students, some of whom took the London
University degree examinations, and in a few cases they attended
university classes. This was the realization of a goal long coveted by
some in the colleges and by others interested in teacher education. One
of the witnesses before the Cross Commission in 1886–8, Canon
Warburton, had said:

> I hope to see a closer approximation of our training college system
> with the liberal culture of the universities, so that all that is best and
> highest in modern education may be brought within the reach of

those to whom the teaching of the great mass of the children of this and coming generations will be entrusted.[5]

This destination was farther off than Canon Warburton thought, but the view was staunchly held by many of his contemporaries. The Board of Education report on colleges for the year 1899 stated that the directors of the provincial universities realized that it was necessary 'to equip the teachers more fully with knowledge of a higher type' and to dispel their narrowness of vision and caste-feeling through more varied curricula and contacts with other students.

And to a large, though still insufficient, extent the action of the day colleges has resulted in effecting this good. Nor has their action stopped short at these limits. It has over-stepped them and has reacted with considerable force upon the residential colleges. It has improved their curricula; it has stirred up emulation – the result of which has been to introduce university studies within their walls, and it is now of yearly occurrence that numbers of their students are prepared for the examination of the London University.[6]

We find this confirmed in many references to the work of the provincial universities and university colleges contained in the reports on those institutions in receipt of grant aid from the central authority. In 1907 the important features of the work of the Education Department at the University of Liverpool were described in the following terms:

In this Department there were 88 women and 76 men. The lectures are open to students of local Training Colleges and to teachers. The statistics show that the percentage of successes in University examinations is large, and that the percentage of failures is relatively small. It is found that the connection between Training College and University has raised the standard of attainment for teachers in primary schools. The intending teacher has to combine his course in Arts with a general course in Science and with professional training. There is, therefore, some danger of over-pressure . . . . Provision is also made for graduate students who intend to be teachers in secondary schools.[7]

The picture is a fairly typical one for this pre-war period.

Thus by the turn of the century a large amount of degree work was being undertaken in men's colleges and a good deal in women's. At one training college in London in 1900 half of the men students were studying for university examinations, and there is evidence from timetables that the major attention was given to their preparation.

> In 1900 the men's colleges, and especially the outstanding London ones, were the poor man's universities, and men of first rate calibre at that time entered the training colleges in face of severe competition and there took degrees.[8]

In the nineteenth century the elementary schools and the education of their teachers had been separate, enclosed systems. With the advent of the day training colleges the education of elementary school teachers for the first time touched the main current of higher education, and for the next twenty years or so it seemed that it might in due course be fully assimilated in the university system. The new local education authority colleges, both county and municipal, had reinforced this tendency. Free from traditional constraints, they sought to provide for their students a better education, better buildings, and better staff with better salaries. Many of them were from the beginning mixed communities of men and women students, like the universities. Their ideal of a better education was conceived in terms of a university degree course. But in the event all these promising developments were checked.

The terms of the Board of Education Regulations of 1918 encouraged the universities and university colleges to concentrate on their four-year courses for graduate students and most of them elected to do so. In fact, the day training colleges had already been undergoing a gradual transformation, becoming fully-fledged departments of education within the universities, and they had gained a wider, though far from universal, respect in higher academic circles. In the day training colleges there was now a sharp decline in the provision of two-year and three-year courses of study for students, whether undergraduate or non-graduate, intending to be teachers. The training colleges were to concern themselves almost entirely with the non-graduate students following a two-year course of study, although one or two retained their graduate courses. Thus the former separation of the colleges from the rest of higher education was largely restored, and prospective graduate and non-graduate teachers attended different institutions. It was unfortunate that this enfranchisement of the colleges was halted just at the time when they were poised to shed their traditional isolation and to assume a more important role in post-secondary education.

Any lingering hopes for the enhancement of the status of the training colleges were dashed by the report of the Departmental Committee on the Training of Teachers in 1925. There was to be no up-grading of the colleges. It said:

> The other main objection to the Training College system which we have to consider is the objection that they [*sic*] segregate teacher-students from others. So far as the universities cannot be expected to receive them (and it will be remembered that there are at present over 4,000 teacher students in training at universities) there appears to be no practicable or desirable alternative to the Training Colleges.[9]

The training colleges were to continue as 'institutions providing normally a two-year course of professional training'. Some lip-service was paid in the report to the desirability of uniting the colleges more closely with the main stream of higher education through co-operation with the universities, but it could not disguise the reality of the cleavage between the two. The Departmental Committee recommended further restrictions upon the colleges. It noted that the choice in academic subjects had been 'almost too encouraging in some instances' and the freedom to pursue the study of chosen subjects to 'a comparatively high point appears sometimes to have absorbed an almost too generous share of energy'. It declared that the business of the two-year colleges was to teach students to be good teachers in elementary schools, and for this purpose they should apply themselves primarily to professional studies.

> We think that the two year courses should become more professional in character and aim, and that the academic work which they include should be undertaken primarily as a means to professional skill, and less for learning or intellectual development in itself . . . .'[10]

It followed from this that there was no room or justification for degree courses in training colleges, and the Departmental Committee recommended their abolition, since the two- or three-year degree course was 'even less defensible' than it had formerly been and they could see no sufficient reason for the continued approval of such an alternative to the four-year degree course. Their proposal was:

> That courses extending over two or three years and comprising a

degree course together with professional training should cease to be recognized as courses qualifying for the Certificate . . . .[11]

The Board of Education implemented these proposals.

The Departmental Committee made some minor suggestions for linking the work of the training colleges with the universities 'through other and different means'. These amounted to a proposal for the delivery of lectures in colleges by visiting university teachers, which seemed preferable to the attendance of college students at the universities, and the possibility of university representation on the governing bodies of colleges. But the affiliation of colleges to universities was rejected.

> To suggestions for 'affiliating' Training Colleges to universities we are not so well disposed . . . . Affiliation otherwise is commonly understood to mean some co-ordination between Training College and university examinations, with the object of giving the College student credit for his attainment should he enter upon a course in the university. This is not an easy matter and we are doubtful whether the results would ever justify the trouble needed to solve practical difficulties.[12]

Finally the Departmental Committee drove home the difference between the colleges and universities by expressing views in favour of single-sex training institutions. The Report declared that mixed colleges for men and women students were more difficult to administer than separate men's colleges and women's colleges, and that any residential colleges established in the future should be for men or women only.

Why did this happen? The principal reason was the Board of Education's inertia and economy in dealing with problems of teacher supply. The desperate need at the end of the nineteenth century and in the early twentieth century had been for a vastly increased number of elementary school teachers. By 1920 this need had been largely met and the day training colleges had done this part of their job well. By 1922 and the following years qualified teachers were experiencing difficulty and delay in obtaining appointments in elementary schools, and the Departmental Committee, in referring to the limitation on college admissions and other measures in 1923, observed that 'over-supply' of teachers would continue to accumulate for another two years at least and 'the over-supply is an over-supply of Certificated Teachers'. The birth-rate continued to fall and its decline was not

E

reversed in the 1930s. In part the retrenchment was due to the pressure of economic circumstances and 'the efforts of the Board and Local Education Authorities to reduce expenditure'. But the trained graduate teachers were still needed for the new secondary schools as the latter grew in size and importance. The middle classes were using the new fee-paying and scholarship opportunities in the secondary schools for the education of their children for a career, and so were many working-class parents. The provincial universities and university colleges could produce these four-year-trained graduate teachers. When in their early years they had been small institutions, struggling to survive, they had been glad to have the two-year and three-year teacher students to swell their numbers and the grant aid that accompanied their presence. But by the 1920s the universities' intake of undergraduate students was much increased and they were less dependent on the income from teacher courses and students. By 1930 the Board of Education and the local authorities estimated that there was a more than adequate supply of trained teachers, both elementary and secondary. The prospect of bringing the training colleges fully into the higher education system had disappeared long before this, however.

The main positive recommendation of the Departmental Committee concerned the final qualifying examination for certificated teachers, which had hitherto been conducted by the Board of Education's inspectors. The Committee thought:

> That the establishment of examining boards should be encouraged, representative of Universities and the Governing Bodies of Training Colleges, to examine the students of a College or group of Colleges for the purpose of the recognition of the students by the Boards as Certificated Teachers.[13]

But even this modest reform was slow to materialize. The Board of Education issued Circular 1373 in December 1925, accepting the Committee's recommendations on the discontinuance of the Board's own Preliminary and Final examinations for teacher students and the replacement of the Final examination by one in the control of which the colleges would have a share. The Board encouraged the formation of joint examining boards, on which university and college interests were represented, and sought proposals from the colleges for alternative methods of examination. By 1928 seven schemes had been drawn up for the 'areas' of: London; Durham University (North); Birmingham University (Midlands); Nottingham University College (Nottinghamshire and Derbyshire); Bristol University (West); Leeds and Sheffield Universities (Yorkshire); and Reading University (South). Manchester and Liverpool Universities and Wales were still outstanding.[14] Cambridge had only one college; Oxford played no part in the scheme. Eventually the joint examining boards got under way and the Board of Education held its Final Examination in academic subjects for the last time in the summer of 1929. But the Board was not prepared to go the whole way in surrendering its control. The H.M.I.s who had had the greatest responsibility for conducting the Certificate Final Examination were allowed to attend the meetings of the joint examining boards, and the Board of Education retained the assessment of teaching practice in its own hands until 1951.

The new joint examining boards and their examinations did not bring the colleges and universities more closely together in a kind of academic partnership, as had been hoped. Indeed it was hardly to be expected that a shared responsibility for examining alone would achieve this. The joint boards framed courses of study and drafted syllabuses for college students; they set examination papers and conducted the Certificate examinations. But these official tasks drew college and university teachers together only occasionally. The informal contacts between the two sides that had been anticipated turned out to be very few, and the colleges did not have the opportunities to benefit from the liberal tone of the universities. In effect, the university connection was illusory. Moreover, the work of the joint examining boards was increasingly subject to criticism. Colleges within the same group were reluctant to develop closer relations with each other, and the Boards did little to rectify this. The disparities between Boards were considerable. The McNair Committee in 1944 criticized their working and achievements, observing that the system was quite unplanned. It summarized its defects by saying that 'the existing arrangements for the recognition, the training, and the supply of teachers are chaotic and ill-adjusted even to present needs'.[15]

The training colleges themselves were anxious to shed the burdens of the past, but they received little encouragement until the post-war years. Major reforms were needed in their organization and procedures, and for these the finances of the colleges were totally inadequate. The McNair Report of 1944 remarked that the majority of the training colleges were small in size, 'many of them being too small for either effective staffing or economical management'. Of 83 recognized training colleges in 1938 there were 64 with fewer than 150 students, and 28 of these had fewer than 100. The Committee's allegation that many colleges were ill equipped and ill housed was supported by damning evidence of inadequacies and dearth of supply. It concluded:

> Such figures are depressing enough, but in the form of totals covering the whole field they fail to reveal the conditions in the most unfortunate of the colleges, in one of which there is no gymnasium, craft room or music room, and the hall, common rooms and art room are inadequate.[16]

The staffs of training colleges were over-burdened by their teaching and supervisory duties, and many of them had no time for the reflection, private reading and research that those working in higher education should rightly pursue. This too was a mark of the history of teacher training and of the poor estimation in which the colleges had been held.

In the post-war situation, however, there was a new spirit abroad in the training colleges, and it was possible to take a fresh look at teacher education. Many of the students entering the colleges after 1945 were older men and women, returning from wartime service, and they helped to enlarge the perspectives of the college communities. The emergency training colleges played a valuable part in this renascence. They were established to meet a crucial post-war need for more teachers and offered a one-year intensive course for students. War service, widely interpreted, was an essential condition of eligibility for admission. Between 1946 and 1951 the emergency scheme yielded a total of approximately 35,000 trained teachers – 23,000 men and 12,000 women.[17] In the early 1950s they came near to constituting one-seventh of the total teaching force in the schools. The emergency colleges achieved a degree of success which rose out of the zealous efforts of staff and students under exacting conditions. Both groups undertook daunting programmes of work, often in the face of adverse circumstances, yet found the experience stimulating and rewarding. Among the adult and experienced students in these colleges there were many with exceptional qualities of character, maturity and sincerity. The emergency training colleges contributed much to the new developments in teaching education, and twenty of them were retained in use as permanent two-year colleges.

All training colleges now began to lose some of their seclusion and were drawn into a closer relationship with the life of the neighbouring community and eventually with the universities, with advantage to both sides. The obsolete restrictions and the grim college regimens were gradually relaxed, and the vigilant supervision of students was ended. Students at training colleges were able to enjoy a freer atmosphere, a richer experience and more varied opportunities than previous generations of students had ever known. More money was made available for teacher education. New colleges were founded, in addition to those emergency colleges which were converted into permanent institutions, and some of these were mixed communities of men and women students.

In the years after the Second World War it was vital that the educational powers and the general public should recognize that education is an investment of national wealth which yields a high and indispensable return. Much of the credit for disseminating this view belongs to the McNair Committee and its co-thinkers. The McNair Report castigated the toleration of the existing elementary school system.

> The truth is that we have not yet emancipated ourselves from the tradition of educating our children on the cheap. We say nothing about the folly of that policy from the point of view of the spiritual heritage of this community and the social justice due to each individual member of the community. But we wish to stress the fact that from the economic point of view it is a short-sighted policy ... and we are persuaded that the material wealth and defensive capacity of a community depend in very high degree upon the kind and quality of education which it gives to its children.[18]

The McNair Report identified the main causes of the torpor and poor standing of the training colleges as concomitants of the general neglect of elementary education.

> The purpose of the training colleges has always been the preparation of teachers for the elementary schools; and the trail of cheapness ... which has dogged the elementary schools has also cast its spell over the training colleges which prepare teachers for them. What is chiefly wrong with the majority of the training colleges is their poverty and all that flows from it.[19]

It was the Committee's strong advocacy that led not only to improvements in the training of teachers but to a growing acceptance by Government and people that education was not merely a service but a public good.

The 1944 Education Act effectively removed the distinction between the old elementary-school and secondary-school systems by substituting a new educational structure, and this reform ended the dualism in the teaching profession. The McNair Committee recommended that the Board should recognize in future only one category of 'qualified teachers', that is to say those with the basic professional qualification and training, and that for all such teachers there should be a single basic salary scale, with appropriate additions. These changes were introduced in 1945 and they helped to remove the long-standing divisions within the profession. The teachers' associations themselves did much to enhance the professional standing of their members. The National Union of Teachers had sedulously fostered the ambitions of the elementary school teachers and would continue to see the advancement of the interests of their members in terms of the achievement of a graduate profession. The four secondary school teacher associations held similar professional aims. The associations concerned with the study and teaching of specialist subjects – the English, Mathematical, Historical, Geographical and Modern Language Associations – promoted contacts between teachers and the universities and they helped to improve their attitudes and professional image. These changes within the teaching profession had an appreciable effect upon the training colleges, seeking to escape from the confines of low status and regard into an assured place in higher education.

The McNair Committee also recommended the establishment of area training authorities with one half of the members advocating the formation of university schools of education for this purpose, while the other half favoured an improved joint board scheme. Both thought the new authorities should be responsible for the curricula, syllabuses and the final assessment of all types of students in training. In the event the pattern for the area training organizations became that of university institutes or schools of education. The Committee also made a number of proposals for the improvement of teacher education, the status of teachers, and the attractiveness of the profession. They included the abolition of the 'pledge' and the system of loans to students operated by some local education authorities; the extension of the normal period of training for non-graduates from two to three years; the raising of the salaries of training college staffs so that they approximated to university salary levels; the secondment of teachers from schools for service in training institutions; the offer by the Board of Education of a number of education fellowships for serving teachers to study the principles and practice of education for one or two years; and the substantial increase of the salaries of teachers in primary and secondary schools. The 'pledge' was abolished in 1951; the salaries of teachers were improved; the three-year course was introduced in 1960. The other proposals made little ground.

The recent expansion of training colleges, particularly within the last decade, has finally transformed them. The impulse that generated the expansion was the need to produce many more teachers in the post-war years and then later to augment teacher supply further in the 1950s and 1960s to cope with the extra children coming into the primary and secondary schools, as a result of the high birth-rate in 1947 and the years immediately following, as well as the tendency for pupils to stay longer at school. Thus it was the school population trends that required the massive expansion of the college in the years between 1964 and 1970. The McNair Committee had noted that there were 83 recognized training colleges at the time of their inquiry, and the total number of students in them was 10,000, while their annual output of trained teachers was 5,000. By 1970 there were 168 colleges with 108,000 students and an annual output of about 38,000 teachers. The Ministry of Education in 1960 took the bold decision to increase the length of the Teacher's Certificate course from two to three years, and there was a year of intermission in 1962 when no qualified teachers left the colleges for the schools. The progressive development of the colleges' resources in buildings, facilities and equipment has therefore been a response to the urgent needs of teacher supply. The changes demanded a heavy total investment from central funds and a remarkable resilience on the part of the colleges themselves. In the process some of the colleges have become large institutions with student populations of a thousand or more. Many more have ceased to be single-sex institutions and have become communities of men and women students, while at the same time some have lost their predominantly residential character by admitting an increasing proportion of day students living in their own homes.

In December 1963 the Lord Robbins Committee on Higher Education proposed that the title of the colleges should be changed from the traditional one of 'training colleges' to that of 'colleges of education' and that a four-year Bachelor of Education degree course should be instituted for selected students in the colleges. The Department of Education and Science sanctioned the change in nomenclature at the end of 1964, but soon afterwards decided that the colleges should remain, for administrative and financial purposes, within the public sector of the binary system of higher education and should not be integrated in university schools of education within the autonomous sector, as the Robbins Report had recommended. In 1965 and the following years many colleges, in conjunction with the universities to which they were affiliated, established four-year courses of study leading to the Bachelor of Education degree. With this innovation the colleges of education at last won back the right to offer their students a degree course, and in this respect the measure of choice which the day training colleges had given their students was restored.

These tonic reforms in the colleges and in the education of teachers have been achieved under the momentum given by the proposals of the McNair and Robbins Committees and also by the pressure from the teachers' own organizations. It has been in the spirit of these proposals that the colleges of education have advanced to their present place in the system of higher education. The McNair Committee shrewdly observed in 1944:

> But there has been an immense improvement in the content and conduct of elementary education during the past forty years; and that improvement is largely due to the education and training given to students in training colleges. And particularly it is due to the devotion of individual men and women on the staff of the colleges who, without an eye to financial reward, and often in the face of difficulties and discouragement, have put before themselves an ideal of service which students, critical as many of them may be, have taken to heart and carried with them into the schools to the lasting benefit of children.[20]

Twenty years later the Robbins Committee made a similar appraisal of the importance and characteristic work of the training colleges.

> The Training Colleges in England and Wales and the Colleges of Education in Scotland alike feel themselves to be only doubtfully recognized as part of the system of higher education and yet to have attained standards of work and a characteristic ethos that justify their claim to an appropriate place in it. The health of the whole public system of education depends upon the efficiency of the colleges; the problem is to define their place in terms of the two aspects of their work; that of providing a general higher education for increasing numbers of young people and that of providing teachers well prepared to meet the changing needs of the schools.[21]

The position could hardly have been put more succintly. Yet the admission of the colleges of education to mature status and the concession of an assured place in higher education have continued to meet opposition.

The reasons for equivocation in some quarters about the role and status of the colleges of education are complex. They lie partly in history, as we have seen, and partly in the fact that several different vested interests converge in any decision about their future – the Department of Education and Science, the maintaining bodies, the universities, the teachers in schools, and the colleges themselves. The recommendation that the colleges should be more closely linked with the universities provoked dissent. The local education authorities did not greet the Robbins and Weaver Reports with much enthusiasm and they spurned the university connection for their own colleges, since it menaced their own control over college finances and teacher recruitment. More surprisingly some elements within the universities belittled the work of the colleges and advocated the severance of their links with the universities, on the pretext that it would be healthy for both parties. Nevertheless this resistance to the claims of the colleges for positive recognition as part of the university branch of higher education was substantial. The Chairman of the Select Committee of the House of Commons on Teacher Training, Mr F. Willey, in discussion with representatives of the colleges in April 1970, remarked:

> If it be a fact that the teachers educated in the colleges are so markedly successful in the schools, then it may well be that, whatever the disadvantages of the colleges, there is something in college of education education which is more relevant to teaching in the schools and more successful in producing results in the schools. If that be so, it would seem to me that, if one is considering higher education, one should give particular attention to this and not submerge the colleges merely in the general case that there should be more higher education.[22]

The desire to maintain the division between the colleges and the main stream of higher education is implicit in this statement. Other more drastic proposals would deny the colleges a genuine part in higher education by detaching them from the universities, and if this were done the whole fabric upon which the development of the colleges had been based since the McNair Report would be dismantled. The most recent discussions on the future of the colleges have not ignored this possibility.

The position of the colleges of education remains vulnerable because they still continue to admit as students only those who intend to become teachers, whether non-graduates or graduates. Historically, this has isolated the colleges from the universities and other institutions of higher education, as we have already seen. The Robbins Committee on Higher Education recognized that most, if not all, of them would in due time become multidiscipline colleges, offering courses of general education as well as teacher training. The Lord James Committee Report indeed proposed that those colleges capable of advancing along these lines should be encouraged to do so, making a start by offering a two-year course of study leading to a Diploma in Higher Education, and it suggested that such 'an expansion would be highly desirable in any case since the colleges would be asked to make important innovations and would be better able to do so in a context of expansion than one of stagnation or contraction'.[23] Later the colleges might, either in conjunction with the universities or not, offer general courses in the 'second cycle' leading to a degree. But the Lord James Committee proposals also embodied a scheme for transferring the academic responsibility for the colleges from the universities to a national council and regional councils for the training and education of teachers. The scene was set for another reversal in the fortunes of the colleges of education which would have renewed their isolation. In the light of the recent White Paper on Education, however, it would seem that the colleges will, on the contrary, be fully assimilated within the system of higher education and, where appropriate, they will offer general courses for non-teacher students in addition to courses of teacher training, both initial and advanced. When this becomes a reality, the colleges may finally shake off the last traces of academic exclusion and disdain under which they have laboured for so long.

The movement for the reform of the training colleges advanced along a slow and daunting path. Unlike the new provincial universities, the colleges were subject to a number of inhibiting forces. They were tied by the Board of Education and by the vagaries of the supply of teachers for the elementary schools, and between 1920 and 1940 the need for elementary school teachers was declining. Their size, character and objectives remained static, and as a result they suffered from a chronically humble reputation. Because they were less eligible places, the colleges came well down the scale for resources. Their place was firmly fixed within the lower ranges of the public sector of the educational system, and the function imposed upon them was an exclusive and narrowly vocational one. It is these distinguishing features that have in the past caused the attribution to the colleges of such low priority and low esteem. Now it seems that at last things may be different. But we can only wonder that such a mistaken policy should have been pursued for so long.

Notes

1   Board of Education, *Report of the Departmental Committee on the Training of Teachers for Public Elementary Schools*, p.9, B.P.P. 1024–5 [Cmnd. 2409] xii, 203.
2   Lance G.E. Jones, *The Training of Teachers in England and Wales* (London, Humphrey Milford, 1924), pp.32–3, 123.
3   Board of Education, *Report for the Year 1912–1913* (London, H.M.S.O., 1914), pp.7–8.
4   Board of Education, *General Reports of H.M. Inspectors of Elementary Schools and Training Colleges for the Year 1902*, p.176, B.P.P. 1903 [Cmnd. 1706] xxi.
5   *Royal Commission on the Working of the Elementary Education Acts (England and Wales)* (Cross Commission), First Report, 1886 [C.4863] xxv.
6   Board of Education, *Report for the Year 1899–1900* (London, H.M.S.O., 1900), Vol. 111, p.334.
7   *Report of the Committee on Grants in Aid to University Colleges*, p.30, B.P.P. 1907 [267] lxiv, 551.
8   Ministry of Education, *Education 1900–1950: Report for the Year 1950* (London, H.M.S.O., 1951), p.82.
9   Board of Education, *Report of the Departmental Committee on the Training of Teachers for Public Elementary Schools*, p.86.
10   Ibid. p.93.
11   Ibid. p.163.
12   Ibid. p.110.
13   Ibid. p.163.
14   Board of Education, *Report for the Year 1926–1927* (London, H.M.S.O., 1928), pp.54–5.
15   Board of Education, *Teachers and Youth Leaders* (Report of the McNair Committee) (London, H.M.S.O., 1944), p.18.
16   Ibid. p.14.
17   Ministry of Education, *Challenge and Response*, Educational Pamphlet 17 (London, H.M.S.O., 1951), p.130.
18   Board of Education, *Teachers and Youth Leaders*, p.31.
19   Ibid. p.13.
20   Board of Education, *Teachers and Youth Leaders*, p.73.
21   Committee on Higher Education, *Higher Education* (Robbins Report) (London, H.M.S.O., 1963) [Cmnd. 2154], p.107.

22   Select Committee on Education and Science, *Teacher Training*, Minutes of Evidence (15 April 1970), pp.390–1, 1970 H.C. (30–xii).
23   Department of Education and Science, *Teacher Education and Training* (Report of the Lord James Committee) (London, H.M.S.O. 1972), pp.75–6.

HAROLD PERKIN

The Professionalization of University Teaching

The title of this paper ought to be the re-professionalization of university teaching, since the original medieval university was a professional training school for theologians, that is, for the professional thinkers and problem-solvers of medieval society. Its founders, Peter Abelard, Duns Scotus, William of Occam and the rest of the 'Schoolmen', were professionals to the core: they invented, or adapted from the Arabs and Greeks, the major tools of thinking which we still use – the dialectical method (thesis, antithesis, synthesis), the economy of hypothesis (Occam's razor), linguistic analysis (grammar), persuasive reasoning (rhetoric), and so on. They soon took on board the other vocational professions as they emerged, notably medicine and the several varieties of law, by the simple device of adding postgraduate faculties. And they rapidly adopted a form of professional organization, to segregate them from the unqualified and protect them from interlopers, which has remained effective down to the twentieth century: the chartered body with its monopoly of awarding degrees. The very words which they used to describe the organization – *universitas, collegium, societas* – were professional words, adapted from the commercial and industrial guild system; and the degrees were simply the levels of professional status, derived also from the guilds – undergraduate or apprentice scholar, bachelor or journeyman scholar, master scholar licensed to practise independently, and doctor or elder scholar, an alderman of the guild or *universitas*.[1]

The medieval universities, then, to which we should add their secular equivalent, the inns of court – graduate schools for secular lawyers – were training schools for all the learned professions – those requiring the ability to read and write the Latin language of learning – and, since such learning was necessary for many aspects of government, increas-

69

ingly for the service of the state as well. This last function saved Oxford and Cambridge from the fate of the monasteries under Henry VIII, who said in their defence:

> I tell you, sir, that I judge no land in England better bestowed than that which is given to our Universities, for by their maintenance our realm shall be well-governed when we be dead and rotten.[2]

Why the universities and inns of court declined into mere finishing schools for young gentlemen, mainly during the sixteenth century, is not my concern here. It has been admirably dealt with by Professor Charlton in his book *Education in Renaissance England*.[3] Their popularity with the sons of the aristocracy and gentry increased as lecturing and examining diminished almost to the point of vanishing – a thought for today's campaign against them – so that by Queen Elizabeth I's day gentlemen's sons at Oxford outnumbered the lower orders by six to five.[4] They seem unlikely to have learned much of a professional kind: most professors did not profess, most readers no longer held readings, most lecturers refused to lecture, and the student who read a book and wrote a paper was lucky if he could find a tutor to hear him read it. At Cambridge, according to William Harrison in 1577, the colleges

> were erected by their founders at first only for poor men's sons, whose parents were not able to bring them up to learning; but now they have the least benefit of them, by reason the rich do so encroach upon them . . . being placed, most of them study little other than histories, tables, dice and trifles . . . . Besides this, being for the most part either gentlemen or rich men's sons, they oft bring the university into much slander. For standing upon their reputation and liberty, they ruffle and roist it out, exceeding in apparel and banting riotous company (which draweth them from their books into another trade), and for excuse, when they are charged with breach of all good order, think it sufficient to say that they be gentlemen, which grieveth many not a little.[5]

The final stage in their decline came after the Civil War and Restoration, when their popularity even as finishing schools – or drinking, gaming and wenching schools – began to sag, and the colleges turned into tiny property-owning oligarchies of leisured fellows – landed gentlemen by appointment, as it were, instead of inheritance – most of them spinning out a reluctant bachelordom while waiting for a

college living in the church to fall vacant. Edward Gibbon found the
'monks of Magdalen', Oxford, 'decent, easy men, who supinely enjoyed
the gifts of the founder.'[6] The undergraduates can be typified by Jack
Egerton, heir to a Cheshire estate, who went to Magdalene, Cambridge,
for a year or two without taking his degree. His mother wrote to him in
1729:

> Your promises aided by my strong affections prove powerful enough
> to make me give in to what you desire [more money], even to forget
> past miscarriages if you'll be serious and make the best use of your
> time you possibly can for the future and study as much as in you lies
> to retrieve the precious time you have unhappily lost. In order to
> that you must drop all the Idle part of your acquaintance and they'll
> not care to trouble you if they find you intent upon a Book. Don't
> make much of your Self in a bad way. No philosopher in Cambridge
> will find occasion for more than four-score pound a Year.[7]

By the eighteenth century, then, university teaching had reached the
nadir of its fortunes as an occupation. One of its leading lights, Adam
Smith, blamed the low pay and status of what he called 'that
unprosperous race of men, commonly called men of letters', on the
overcrowding of the market for teachers by cheap, subsidized education, only mitigated by the job opportunities of a still more inferior
market, for Grub Street journalists:

> The time and study, the genius, knowledge and application requisite
> to qualify an eminent teacher of the sciences, are at least equal to
> what is necessary for the greatest practitioners in law and physic.
> But the usual reward of the eminent teacher bears no proportion to
> that of the lawyer or physician: because the trade of the one is
> crowded with indigent people who have been brought up to it at the
> public expense; whereas those of the other two are encumbered with
> very few who have not been educated at their own. The usual
> recompense, however, of public and private teachers, small as it may
> appear, would undoubtedly be less than it is, if the competition of
> those yet more indigent men of letters who write for bread was not
> taken out of the market. Before the invention of the art of printing,
> a scholar and a beggar seem to have been terms nearly synonymous.
> The different governors of the universities before that time appear to
> have often granted licences to their scholars to beg.

He goes on, still more topically, in a way which would gladden

Mrs Thatcher's heart:

> This inequality is upon the whole, perhaps, rather advantageous than hurtful to the public. It may somewhat degrade the profession of a public teacher; but the cheapness of literary education is surely an advantage which greatly overbalances this trifling inconveniency. The public too might derive still greater benefit from it, if the constitution of these schools and colleges, in which education is carried on, was more reasonable than it is at present through the greater part of Europe.[8]

It is often claimed that Scottish education in general and Scottish universities in particular were not so moribund and amateurish as the English, and certainly the movement for reform of the profession was to begin there, amongst the friends and pupils of Adam Smith at Glasgow and at Edinburgh. But their superiority has been misunderstood and exaggerated, since they were primarily engaged in providing the secondary education which in England was provided by the endowed grammar and public schools. As late as 1823 *Blackwood's Edinburgh Magazine* remarked of the largest of them:

> The University of Glasgow is composed of two things; first, a school where boys from twelve years of age up to sixteen or seventeen, are instructed in the elements of Classical learning – for they do not know even the *alphabet* of the Greek tongue when they are matriculated – and also, in the first elements of Mathematics, Logic, Ethics, etc.; and secondly, of an institution in which lectures are delivered on Medicine, Law and Theology for the benefit of those of rather riper years .... The boys who attend the school wear red frieze gowns – and miserable filthy little urchins the far greater part of them are. To dream of comparing them with the boys of Eton, or Westminster, or Winchester, or Harrow, either in regard to appearance, or manners, or what is of higher importance than all, in regard to SCHOLARSHIP, would be about as absurd, as it would be to compare a Spouting Club in Cheapside with the British House of Commons.[9]

In Adam Smith's day, however, the social revolution which was ultimately to lead to the professionalization not only of university teaching but also of most of the non-manual occupations of modern society had already begun. The Industrial Revolution was undoubtedly the main driving force behind the reform of the old universities and the founding of new ones, as it was behind the reform of the old professions like medicine and the law and the founding of vast numbers of new ones, from engineers of every kind, through architects, surveyors, dental surgeons, pharmacists, chemists, physicists and the like to chartered company secretaries, accountants, insurance officials, and even interior decorators and photographers. These have been admirably chronicled by Geoffrey Millerson in *The Qualifying Associations*.[10] Industrialism operated very indirectly on the universities, since at first the universities were totally irrelevant to industrialism. Their function was the conservation of ancient scholarship, not the discovery of new knowledge, and scarcely one of the great inventions and discoveries that made the modern world was made in a university, until at least the closing decades of the nineteenth century. The Hunter brothers in surgery, Jenner in medicine, Priestley in chemistry, Bentham in law and government, Malthus in population studies, James Mill and Ricardo in economics, Davy and Faraday in physics, Darwin in biology, Sir George Cayley in aeronautics, Thomas Wedgwood in the discovery of light-sensitive chemicals which led to photography and, it goes without saying, the whole gamut of practical inventors in textiles and metallurgy, from Arkwright and Crompton to Nasmyth and Bessemer, operated entirely outside the universities. Two exceptions prove the rule: James Watt was given laboratory space in Glasgow University to prevent his eviction by the City Corporation – but this was by the individual patronage of Professor Joseph Black, and Watt was in no sense a university don or research assistant; and the Rev. Edmund Cartwright, inventor of the power loom, a wool-combing machine, a quadricycle and an alcohol engine (forerunners of the bicycle and the internal combustion engine), was sometime fellow of Magdalen College, Oxford – but he resigned to marry an heiress long before he took to inventing.[11]

Yet these inventions and discoveries, so remote from the ivory towers of the dons, were destined so to transform society that it would come to demand a totally different university system and a new kind of university teaching profession to service it – or rather, two systems, one completely new and one a reformed version of the old, with two almost incompatible professions to staff them. Both systems were to fuse in the twentieth century into a single one, with important elements contributed by each to a single profession.

The new system was new only for England. It had its roots in the Scottish universities and, through them, in the main European tradition

F

of university education. It was the professorial tradition of scholarship and research, of the dedicated scholar who found time to share his abundance of learning and discovery with a small band of student apprentices. It was oriented towards the real world and its problems, whether scientific, technological or social, and it stressed the vocational element of education, both in the sense of a serious call to the life of scholarship and in the sense of being relevant to the student's particular career. The tradition, never quite dead in Scotland, was revived in the eighteenth century, by Adam Smith and his teachers and pupils of the 'Scottish historical school of philosophy' – Adam Ferguson, Dugald Stewart, William Robertson, John Millar and the rest – who in effect founded the modern social sciences, notably economics, historical sociology, the statistical analysis of society, and that economic interpretation of history and government which so influenced Marx.[1][2] There was also a very practical school of applied science, characterized by Watt's patron, Joseph Black, professor at Glasgow and later at Edinburgh, where he laid the foundations of the modern schools of medicine and chemistry.

Into England the new system was imported by graduates of Edinburgh University, led by Thomas Campbell, James Mill and Henry Brougham, who with their Whig and dissenting friends founded University College, London, in 1826. This was a response to the demand by the expanding middle class for a university, education, cheaper and more relevant to their needs than the ancient learning of Oxbridge. The first chairs, half of them filled by Scots, included medicine, law, political economy, logic, philosophy, modern languages, chemistry, natural philosophy (physics), engineering (not filled till 1841), mineralogy, industrial design and education – the whole spectrum of a modern university curriculum with the deliberate exception of theology. James Bryce began the first training of teachers there in 1836. The medical school was the lynch-pin of the enterprise – three out of four students (347 out of 469) in 1834 were medicals – showing the direct pressure of the demand of the new industrial society for professional service. Medical schools were in fact the leading shoot of the new growth, and no less than 60 of them were founded in various towns, as against 29 general colleges, down to 1851. The more important of these medical schools and local colleges evolved, often by amalgamation, into the new civic universities of later Victorian and Edwardian England, notably in Manchester, Liverpool and Leeds (the Victoria University, 1880), Birmingham (1898), Sheffield (1905),

Newcastle (1908) and Bristol (1909), and the University Colleges of Nottingham (1881), Reading (1892), Exeter (1893) and Southampton (1902). All these followed in the professorial steps of Scotland and London.[13]

So too did the foundations of the Tory-Anglican counter-movement. King's College, London, opened its doors in 1831 with even lower fees than the rival 'Godless college in Gower Street', and with equally professional and vocational courses, including by 1840 medicine, engineering and architecture, and with an impressive staff of professors which included J.F. Daniell, inventor of the hygrometer and constant electric battery, Sir Charles Wheatstone, inventor of the electric telegraph, and Sir Charles Lyell, whose geological theories, despite his own orthodox opinions, did more to undermine traditional belief in the Biblical version of Creation than anything emanating from the 'Godless college'. Durham University (1833), a truly Church foundation designed to pre-empt criticism and perhaps sequestration of the vast wealth of the dean and chapter, was a collegiate structure consciously imitative of Oxford, but with its own quota of teaching professors and modern subjects, including chemistry, mineralogy and engineering.[14]

Yet this proliferation of middle-class universities in the industrial and growing commercial cities in no way derogated from the primacy of Oxford and Cambridge which, indeed, came to supply most of their professors. Their dons and students, too, remained at least as numerous in 1900 as those of the rest of the English universities put together.[15] The professionalization of university teaching, therefore, required still more the reform of Oxford and Cambridge, which in fact accompanied and even to a large extent preceded the founding of the civic universities. There the movement for reform could scarcely come from the 'inert, almost moribund professoriate', since, though some professors like Arnold at Oxford and Sedgwick at Cambridge played a leading role, they were too few and too powerless to transform the old universities into Scottish or Continental professorial institutions. The tradition there, evolved through centuries of playing bear-leader to recalcitrant and often anti-intellectual gilded youth, was of the college tutor, the guide, philosopher and friend, rather the learned doctor, of the undergraduate, who looked to him for the formation of character and a gentlemanly way of life rather than learning and a dedicated career of scholarship. Under such model tutors as Benjamin Jowett at Oxford and Oscar Browning of Cambridge the tutorial tradition was elevated to the fine art of raising Christian gentlemen with a moral concern for the less fortunate classes and a determination to serve society and the Empire. It was a noble tradition which did much to put a touch of altruism and *noblesse oblige* back into the selfishness of the Victorian gospel of self-help, which indeed it was intended to: Oxbridge's determination to civilize and save the souls of barbarian aristocrat and philistine bourgeois alike.

The connection between industrialism and the reform of Oxford and Cambridge is tenuous enough. The bludgeonings of the Whiggish *Edinburgh Reviewers* and the Radical *Westminster Review* and *Quarterly Journal of Education* merely put the universities on the defensive, as did the nonconformist campaign of James Heywood, the Manchester M.P., in the 1840s. It was only when a sufficient body of young tutors inside the sacred walls took up the cry — heard faintly from outside — that anything was done. Mark Pattison said of 1850: 'A restless fever of change had spread through the Colleges — the wonder-working phrase "University Reform" had been uttered and that in the House of Commons. The sound seemed to breathe new life into us.'[16] It still took two Acts of parliament (Oxford 1854, Cambridge 1856) and two Executive Commissions to open them to non-Anglican students, to give the universities some real functions over against the colleges, and to reorganize the professoriate. And it took further Acts and Commissions, in 1871–2 and 1877, to abolish religious tests and the celibacy rule for dons and put the relations between the universities and colleges on a reasonable footing.[17] The social cost was considerable, too, in the abolition of the poverty clauses for most scholarships and awards, which opened them to 'merit' of the kind acquired at public schools, thus ensuring that the next half-century saw fewer poor students at Oxford and Cambridge than at any time in their history.[18] Nevertheless, new subjects were introduced, especially science, laboratories built, and Oxford and Cambridge began to become modern universities offering almost as wide a range of courses as the Scottish and civic, though retaining their idiosyncratic tutorial methods both of teaching and paternal care. At the end of the process the old universities had, like the public schools before them, been transformed, but not into mere training schools for the new capitalist bourgeoisie. Rather had the sons of the bourgeoisie been converted to the aristocratic, classically oriented values of Oxford and Cambridge.[19] Indeed, it might be said that two of the most significant features of late Victorian England, the smooth transition from an aristocratic to a plutocratic society dominated by a wealthy business class with traditional paternalist ideas, and the not unconnected decline of the innovating entrepreneurial drive of British industry, were largely derived from the 'civilization' of the high capitalist middle class by the public schools and the old universities.

By 1900, then, both new systems had come into being, and there had been an explosion of student numbers. In England and Wales numbers had grown from 1,128 in 1800 and 5,500 as late as 1885 to 16,735 in 1899.[20] But the profession was still tiny – less than 2,000 university teachers in Great Britain, nearly half of them in Oxford and Cambridge – and the degree of professionalization was minimal. The fellows of the Oxbridge colleges were still, in spite of the leaven of married dons, Nonconformists and scientists, recognizably the gentlemen amateurs they had always been. And in Scotland and the English and Welsh provinces (including London) there was no recognized career structure: the lucky few (31.4 per cent in 1910) were professors,[21] all the rest underpaid assistants, for the most part without tenure or prospect of promotion. And, outside Oxford and Cambridge with between 400 and 500 dons each, they were mostly scattered in tiny groups: Manchester, the largest, had only 67 academic staff, 24 of them professors,[22] and most had less than half that number. More important, although a host of new and especially vocational subjects had been established in the universities, in no profession with the exception of medicine was it essential to have a university degree, and the vast majority of business and professional men were non-graduates.

How did university teaching (and its recent offshoots in other higher education institutions) become what I have called elsewhere the 'key profession', the profession which selects and educates, and increasingly also does the fundamental research for, the other professions?[23]

Some people, of course, would deny that it is a profession at all – at best a collection of bits of professions, assembled on the principle that those who can, do, and those who can't, teach. But professions in this very professional century come in all shapes and sizes, and few of them fit all the criteria of the classic ancient professions of the law, physic and the clergy: the specialized intellectual training, the expert technique or learned 'mystery', the fixed remuneration by fee or stipend, the sense of responsibility for the fiduciary service which the client or public must take on trust, the closed association or exclusive club which protects the public and disciplines members, and over all the legal monopoly granted by the State.[24] But then all the emerging professions and quasi-professions aspire to these criteria, and we should rather think of a rising scale of professionalism than a definitive cluster of indispensable attributes.[25] On this scale university teaching is not so advanced as the law and medicine, or any of the registered professions such as architects, mining engineers or midwives, but it is considerably more advanced than the civil service, the bank clerks, the management professions (with the exception of accountants) and (until the teaching certificate finally does become compulsory), the school-teaching profession.

The academic profession is now in practice developing a specialized training, however inappropriate to half of the job (the Ph.D.); an expert technique, however ill-acquired (teaching by lecture and tutorial and research in libraries and archives or laboratories); a fixed remuneration in the form of national salary scales binding on the individual institutions; a fiduciary service which the clients (the student for teaching and the public for research) are increasingly disposed to question, but in the end still have to take on trust; a closed but not quite comprehensive association, the Association of University Teachers, which accepts only staff in F.S.S.U. grades and has a monopoly of negotiating rights at both national and local levels; and, if not a legal monopoly of the occupation, at least a form of tenure for all those who have completed three or four years' service which is the envy of most other professions.

How did the profession of university teaching acquire these wide functions, responsibilities and rights? How did it become the key profession of the twentieth century?

First, there has been the vast expansion in the size of the profession and the demand for its services. From less than 2,000 members on the eve of the First World War and less than 5,000 on the eve of the Second, it grew to about 15,000 at the time of the Robbins Report (1963) and to about 30,000 today.[26] This enormous growth reflects two connected features of modern industrial society: the growing popular demand for higher education, or at least for the paper qualifications which are increasingly the passport to high status and income (even though the race for them could become, but has not yet, self-defeating), and the growing demand from business and the professions for trained personnel who, increasingly it seems, can no longer be trained by business and the professions themselves. One has only to glance at the list of subjects now commonly taught in universities which were unknown or rare before the war – from sociology or the Hayter area studies to computer science and business studies – to realize how much of the world's work is now taught and researched into there. Indeed, *pace* the claims of the polytechnics, there is no subject or vocation with a substantial intellectual content which is not taught and studied in some British university.

Secondly, they now reach and influence a much larger fraction of society than ever before. It is not merely that they teach much larger numbers of students – about 240,000 today as against about 50,000 before the war and a peak of about 85,000 after it (1949–50) – and will teach still more, even by Mrs Thatcher's reduced estimate, by 1981 (375,000); or that the percentage of the age group going to university has risen from under 1 per cent in 1900, under 2 per cent between the wars and only 4 per cent at the Robbins Report to 8 per cent today, and will rise to 11 per cent by 1981.[27] Nor is it that the real undergraduate population is much larger than that, and must include all those taking degrees in polytechnics, technical colleges and colleges of education, and the Open University – the figures are hard to come by, but they would probably raise the percentage of the age group now to 10 per cent or more and by 1981 to something approaching 20 per cent[28] – or that the vast majority of the staffs of the non-university colleges are themselves products of the university sector. It is the much more significant fact that there is now scarcely a profession or white-collar occupation whose upper echelons are not staffed by graduates, with the partial exception of the trade unions and the entertainment industry. Even the police and the armed forces are advertising for their quota, and paying recruits while they go to college or university. Leaving aside the economic and social spin-off in improved living standards, health and environment from university research, and the cultural spin-off from the books, articles, television and radio programmes by university dons, 'pretty well every person in the country', to quote Halsey and Trow, 'is moulded, directly or indirectly, by university training.'

Thirdly, universities individually are now much larger and more complex institutions than they were. Up to the time of the Robbins Report the majority of universities and university colleges had less than 2,000 students, and the largest outside Oxford and Cambridge (about 9,000 each) had about 6,000. The new universities with their plans for a 'minimum viable size' of 3,000 students were then thought to be overweeningly ambitious. Now the giants of yesterday have become the norms of today, the largest universities are 12,000 or 13,000 and still growing, and even modest new and expanding universities think nothing of plans for 10,000. In terms of staff this means that most universities ten years ago had less than 250 academic staff, and only a handful had over 500. Today, staffs of 500-plus are commonplace, and ones of 1,000-plus becoming familiar. With this increase in size, a profound change has taken place in the atmosphere and organization of universities. Old, informal means of communication have broken down and have had to be replaced by increasingly formal, institutionalized ones: hierarchies of committees, a veritable blizzard of duplicated paper, a whole new bureaucracy of administrators with career patterns and professional problems of their own, formal journals or house magazines to maintain contact between the central administration and the outlying staff, and so on. And the introduction of much wider representation for junior staff and students has increased the formality, the number of committees and the frequency of meetings. Leaving aside the growing pains of staff discontent and student unrest which have come with increased size, university administration for both administrators and academics has become big business, operating large management functions and controlling expenditure ranging from £3 to £20 million a year. At the same time single departments have become as large in staff and student numbers and in budgetary scale as whole faculties used to be, and senior academics have increasingly been forced to become managers and administrators rather than merely teachers, with consequent changes, by no means all for the better, in their relations with their junior colleagues and students. We have now reached the point where universities are seriously discussing sending professors and other heads of department on management courses.

Along with this, fourthly, the built-in tendency in all expanding human institutions towards hierarchy has shown itself. At the beginning of the century, as we have seen, nearly a third of all university teachers were professors. Between the wars, the proportion shrank to about one-fifth. Since the war it has declined still further, to about one in nine or ten.[29] But even this does not gauge the extent of the trend: there is a higher top emerging in the shape of 'super-professors', heads of department, deans of school and the like. (In the polytechnics and technical colleges, always more hierarchical in tendency, the trend has gone much further, and they are top-heavy with non-teaching heads of departments, schools and divisions, permanent deans, deputy principals, and so on.) There is now a strong, anti-authoritarian counter-current, demanding departmental democracy, rotating chairmanships, and the reduction of hierarchy generally, but whether it will effectively overcome the powerful drive, common to all professions, towards domination by the professionally most successful and prestigious, may well be doubted. Indeed, a purely democratic profession is a contradiction in terms: professions only exist because some men know more or are more skilled than others, and if it were not so the profession would have nothing to offer the public. Democracy in all non-academic matters and consultation in all academic ones are the order of the day, but a university in which the students and junior staff were already as knowledgeable as their seniors would have nothing to teach them, and might just as well shut up shop.

Fifthly, as one might expect, the demand for longer training and more paper qualifications which is such a feature of modern society has naturally affected the chief providers of qualifications, and university teachers are better qualified in terms of higher degrees than they were. It is now extremely rare for a young lecturer to be appointed without either a Ph.D. or the prospect of one, and certainly without five or six years of higher education (that is one reason why there are so few women in the profession, since women are so reluctant to spend two or three of their most marriageable years doing research). Whether they are better qualified in the true sense of being intellectually superior is another question: with the expansion the proportion of firsts amongst new entrants (if that means anything) has gone down from three-quarters before 1945 and two-thirds between 1945 and 1959, to less than half in 1960–8.[30]

Finally, the increasing professionalism of the university teacher has expressed itself, as in other rising professions, in the demand for a professional organization with real influence over the terms, conditions and standards of the profession's life and work. The Association of University Teachers grew out of an association of lecturers caught by the inflation and lagging real incomes of the First World War. It was founded in 1919 when the lecturers and professors were forced into an alliance to protect their superannuation. For fifty years it remained a professional pressure group, with some influence on the universities mainly through their relations with the Vice-Chancellors' Committee and their pressure on the State through the University Grants Committee and the Treasury, but with no real power.[31] Suddenly, in the last few years its position has been transformed. In the space of a couple of years, between 1970 and 1972, it became a registered trade union, it negotiated real negotiating powers over salaries and related matters with the University Authorities Panel and the Department of

Education and Science, and it came to be recognized as 'sole bargaining agent' in every university except Oxford and Cambridge (where the difficulty is to discover with whom to negotiate). It is still of course an uneasy coalition of professors and non-professors, whose interests, for example over narrower or wider salary differentials between the lecturers' grade and the professorial average, are often in conflict, and from time to time one or the other group threatens to secede and set up on its own or join a rival union. But on the whole the vast majority recognize that there is more strength in unity than in fragmentation, and the forces of cohesion are greater than those of dissolution. Its greatest achievement has not been in the field of salaries or super-annuation, or even in the pressure towards an expanded and integrated higher education system, but in the establishment of tenure, in a shorter qualifying period and on better terms than any other university system or almost any other profession.

There are even signs that it is beginning to pull together the two separate traditions of the academic profession. For fifty years the fellows of Oxford and Cambridge, with their medieval corporate privileges and guild masters' equality, felt little need for the protection and support of the A.U.T. But recently, with the cold winds of change blowing from the State through the corridors of the D.E.S. and the U.G.C., they have begun to see the value of professional solidarity and have begun to join the Association in larger numbers. At the same time, the gentlemanly dons, especially in the natural and social sciences, have begun to become much more professional, more like their colleagues in other universities, and indeed, with more interchange, much the same people. Conversely, the introduction over the last twenty years of the tutorial system, both in the form of teaching in small groups and in the shape of paternal care (one of the paradoxes of this age of aggressively adult students) in the other universities, has made the Oxbridge don indistinguishable from the university teacher elsewhere. Of course, given the in-built snobbery of English society and still more of the English education system, the sense of effortless superiority — effortless? superiority? — will die hard.

Meanwhile, the most important decision facing the profession and the A.U.T. will be to determine whether to make a takeover bid for all the academics teaching to degree level in the non-university colleges, or whether to maintain the principle that the unique characteristic of the university teacher is the combination of teaching and research at the frontiers of knowledge. Whatever it decides, there can be no doubt that university teaching is now nothing like the tiny, isolated and dispersed, and almost irrelevant occupation it was at the beginning of this century. It has become not merely *a* profession, but *the* profession towards which all the rest must look for the supply of new recruits and of new ideas, on which the future of our society depends.

Notes

1   Hastings Rashdall, *Universities of Europe in the Middle Ages*, new ed., edited by F.M. Powicke and A.B. Emden, 3 vols (Oxford, Clarendon Press, 1936), *passim*.
2   Quoted in Albert Mansbridge, *The Older Universities of Oxford and Cambridge* (London, Longmans, 1923), p.50.
3   Kenneth Charlton, *Education in Renaissance England* (London, Routledge and Kegan Paul, 1965), *passim*.
4   Ibid. p.136
5   William Harrison, *Description of England* (1577; ed. L. Withington, 1876), pp.252–3.
6   Edward Gibbon, *Autobiography* (Oxford, 1907 ed.), pp.36, 40.
7   Mrs E. Egerton, to John Egerton, 25 March 1729, Egerton MSS, Tatton Park.
8   Adam Smith, *The Wealth of Nations* (1776; ed. E.B. Bax, 1905), I, pp.138, 140.
9   'Vindiciae Gallicae', *Blackwood's Edinburgh Magazine*, XIII (1823), p.94.
10 Geoffrey Millerson, *The Qualifying Associations* (London, Routledge and Kegan Paul, 1964), esp. chronological list, pp.246–54.
11 Samuel Smiles, *Lives of the Engineers* (1866 ed.), IV, pp.105–6; *Dictionary of National Biography*, IX, pp.221 f.
12 Cf. R.L. Meek, 'The Scottish contribution to Marxist sociology', in John Saville (ed.), *Democracy and the Labour Movement* (London, Lawrence and Wishart, 1954).
13 Cf. W.H.G. Armytage, *Civic Universities* (London, Benn, 1955), pp.173–6, 224–5.
14 Loc. cit.
15 A.H. Halsey and Martin Trow, *The British Academics* (London, Faber, 1971), pp.145, 151–3.
16 Quoted in Mansbridge, op. cit. p.156.
17 Cf. A.I. Tillyard, *A History of University Reform* (Cambridge, Heffer, 1913), Chs vi-ix; Sheldon Rothblatt, *The Revolution of the Dons: Cambridge and Society in Victorian England* (London, Faber, 1968), Part II; Brian Simon, *Studies in the History of Education, 1780–1880* (London, Lawrence and Wishart, 1960), pp.84–94; 281–99.
18 Mansbridge, op. cit. pp. 108–9; Hester Jenkins and D. Caradog Jones, 'Social class of Cambridge University alumni of 18th and 19th centuries', *British Journal of Sociology* (1950), I, pp.93 f.
19 Cf. Rothblatt, op. cit. Epilogue.

20   Mansbridge, op.cit. p.xxii; Armytage, op cit. p.223; A.N. Little, 'Some myths of university expansion', *Sociological Studies in British University Education*, Sociological Review Monograph No. 7 (Keele University, 1963), p.196.
21   Halsey and Trow, op. cit. p.153.
22   H.B. Charlton, *Portrait of a University* (Manchester, 1951), p.183.
23   Harold Perkin, *Key Profession: the History of the Association of University Teachers* (London, Routledge and Kegan Paul, 1969).
24   Cf. A.M. Carr-Saunders and P.A. Wilson, *The Professions* (Oxford, Clarendon Press, 1933), pp.284–7.
25   Cf. W.E. Moore, *The Professions: Roles and Rules* (New York, Russell Sage Foundation, 1970), esp. Ch. 1..
26   University Grants Committee figure for the main grades in 1971–2 is 28,840; with research and other full-time ancillary academic staff it would be in excess of 32,000.
27   Cf. *Education: a Framework for Expansion*, p.35 (London, H.M.S.O., 1972), Cmnd. 5174; *Higher Education: Report of Robbins Committee*, p.16 (London, H.M.S.O., 1963), Cmnd. 2154.
28   The White Paper figures for all students in higher education rise from 15 per cent of the age group in 1971 to 22 per cent in 1981, but what proportion of these will be on degree courses is still unclear – *Education: a Framework for Expansion*, p.35.
29   Halsey and Trow, op. cit. pp.151–3.
30   Cf. Perkin, op. cit. Table 6, p.260.
31   Ibid. *passim*.

Index

85

For Product Safety Concerns and Information please contact our EU
representative GPSR@taylorandfrancis.com
Taylor & Francis Verlag GmbH, Kaufingerstraße 24, 80331 München, Germany

www.ingramcontent.com/pod-product-compliance
Lightning Source LLC
Chambersburg PA
CBHW061836220326
41599CB00027B/5301